101
WAYS TO

Study Easier and Faster

By: Melanie Falconer

COLLEGE STUDY HACKS: 101 WAYS TO STUDY EASIER AND FASTER

1405 SW 6th Avenue • Ocala, Florida 34471 • Phone 800-814-1132 • Fax 352-622-1875

Website: www.atlantic-pub.com • Email: sales@atlantic-pub.com

SAN Number: 268-1250

Library of Congress Cataloging-in-Publication Data

Names: Falconer, Melanie.

Title: College study hacks : 101 ways to study easier and faster / by Melanie Falconer.

Description: Ocala, Florida : Atlantic Publishing Group, Inc., [2016] | Includes bibliographical references and index.

Identifiers: LCCN 2016059527 (print) | LCCN 2017002213 (ebook) | ISBN 9781620231913 (pbk. : alk. paper) | ISBN 1620231913 (alk. paper) | ISBN 9781620232446 (library edition : alk. paper) | ISBN 9781620231920 (ebook)

Subjects: LCSH: Study skills. | College student orientation.

Classification: LCC LB2395 .F285 2017 (print) | LCC LB2395 (ebook) | DDC 378.1/7--dc23

LC record available at https://lccn.loc.gov/2016059527

Printed in the United States

PROJECT MANAGER: Rebekah Sack • rsack@atlantic-pub.com

ASSISTANT EDITORS: Yvonne Bertovich and Cathie Bucci

INTERIOR LAYOUT AND JACKET DESIGN: Nicole Sturk • nicolejonessturk@gmail.com

COVER DESIGN: Jackie Miller • millerjackiej@gmail.com

Reduce. Reuse.
RECYCLE.

A decade ago, Atlantic Publishing signed the Green Press Initiative. These guidelines promote environmentally friendly practices, such as using recycled stock and vegetable-based inks, avoiding waste, choosing energy-efficient resources, and promoting a no-pulping policy. We now use 100-percent recycled stock on all our books. The results: in one year, switching to post-consumer recycled stock saved 24 mature trees, 5,000 gallons of water, the equivalent of the total energy used for one home in a year, and the equivalent of the greenhouse gases from one car driven for a year.

Over the years, we have adopted a number of dogs from rescues and shelters. First there was Bear and after he passed, Ginger and Scout. Now, we have Kira, another rescue. They have brought immense joy and love not just into our lives, but into the lives of all who met them.

We want you to know a portion of the profits of this book will be donated in Bear, Ginger and Scout's memory to local animal shelters, parks, conservation organizations, and other individuals and nonprofit organizations in need of assistance.

*— **Douglas & Sherri Brown,***
President & Vice-President of Atlantic Publishing

Table of Contents

Introduction

The college freshman walks onto campus with their new set of folders, notebooks, and studying utensils. Maybe they're slinging a brand new backpack, nodding ever-so-slyly at the booths for campus organizations, hoping that they're blending in on their first day. Their college professors gave them summer homework, and guess what? They nailed it, and it's freshly printed, ready to be handed in on the first day. What they don't know is that it takes a lot more than fresh materials and confidence to be ready for the challenges that college inevitably presents.

Most freshmen prepare for many changes in this new chapter of their lives, but don't expect the real obstacles facing them. College isn't just a series of classes "harder" than high school and a couple of parties every week. College demands that a student takes full ownership of their education and dedicates themselves to knowledge and critical thinking. Being that quiet kid in the classroom who skates by on last-minute assignments won't slide. Staying home from class and looking up information on Wikipedia to complete assignments won't work, either. Why? College doesn't have short cuts. It's a whole new universe, and that's essential to know from day one.

The statistics don't lie. According to a 2016 report from the National Center for Education Statistics, more than 40 percent of first-time full-time students who enroll in a bachelor's degree program don't graduate within 6 years. More statistics show that even the most successful high school students can have difficulties succeeding in a university setting. The same students who received flawless AP or SAT scores are sometimes the same students who struggled to maintain a 2.0 GPA in their postsecondary education. Yes—even the most intelligent students *can* fail in college.

The reason for this is two-fold. Studying isn't a natural inclination in the same way that we seek to feed ourselves or socialize with friends and family. Many of us need to use discipline for us to sit down and hit the books. Furthermore, the study skills and techniques necessary to succeed in high school are sometimes entirely different from those in college. This isn't to say that college students need to forget previous methods of studying; they just need to adapt.

The second reason why students struggle is because some students are shocked by the workload. They are overwhelmed by what is expected from them and go to one extreme or the other: they become the party animal or the perfectionist.

College graduates, on average, earn more over the course of their careers than non-graduates, so it's imperative that freshmen learn how to be successful students. Studying in college isn't just a mindless activity like rote memorization or making note cards. Successful studying is a lifestyle, designed for an individual, by an individual, to help him or her have a well-rounded college education.

Even though each student has a unique learning style, the most successful college students have some of the following attributes:

Proactive Learning. Simply reading over information that will be on an exam or quiz is not enough to receive a high grade in a college-level course. Proactive learners take the initiative to read, write, think, and talk about the subject so they know and understand the material. Professors want their students to become fluid, open, and independent thinkers—not mindless robots with a repeat button.

Self-awareness. Successful college students have a high level of self-awareness when it comes to studying. They know what subjects will sit well with their brains, and which ones throw them into chaos. They know *when* they're at their best and *how* to study at their best—whether through journaling, reading outside materials, or talking with other students.

Motivation. Motivation keeps a student going when college life becomes stressful. This perseverance includes attending class (yes, even if it's at 8 a.m.), keeping up with assigned reading material, and putting in hard work when the class calls for it.

Many college students don't naturally have these characteristics — these are learned skills. No one was ever "born" to be a great college student. However, this book covers tips and tricks necessary for success that teach active learning strategies, promote self-awareness, and foster motivation.

This book isn't designed for textbook reading. Instead, it's like a tour guide, showing you the way when you're lost in a new place, and all you want to do is sit down on the curb, cry, and eat some pizza. There will be times when you struggle with a course like "Phonetic Analysis" or "The Dissolution of Existentialism in Post-War France" and you don't have the skills to jump over the obstacles that crop up. This book contains strategies that are proven time and time again not just for students to get an "A" in their class, but to study effectively so they can enjoy life!

After an initial read-through, the book can be used as a point-by-point resource to help college students stay on track. It's a reference guide for when you just don't know where to go, and again, all you want is some pizza.

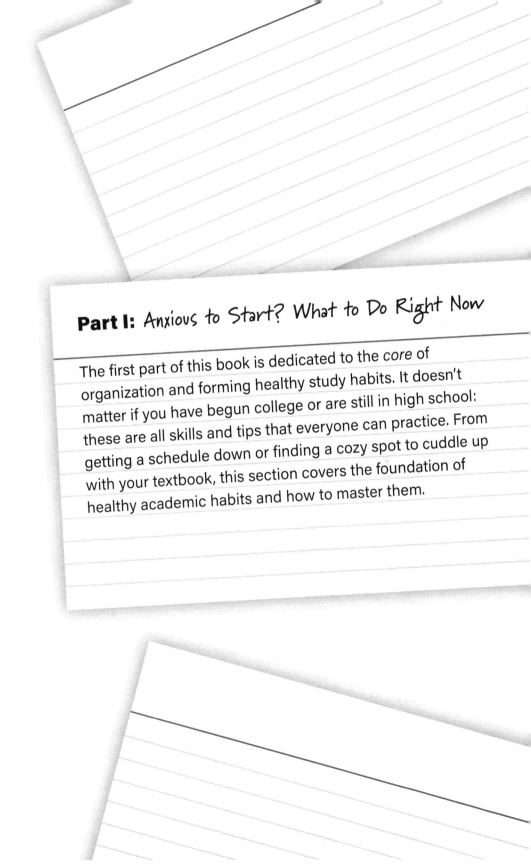

Part I: Anxious to Start? What to Do Right Now

The first part of this book is dedicated to the *core* of organization and forming healthy study habits. It doesn't matter if you have begun college or are still in high school: these are all skills and tips that everyone can practice. From getting a schedule down or finding a cozy spot to cuddle up with your textbook, this section covers the foundation of healthy academic habits and how to master them.

Crafting an Ideal Schedule

A successful student is a schedule artisan who has managed their time so that, even at their busiest, they can stay on top of work and also have time to relax, unwind, and have fun. The untrained schedule artisan has put down their brush and embraced the chaos of not knowing what's next—whether it be getting hit on the head with a term paper or smacked with an unanticipated deadline or a seemingly impossible project. In college, crafting the ideal schedule is an art that *needs* to be perfected if you want any hope for success.

Here are some signs that tell you whether or not you need to use a scheduling system:

- You wake up on top of the book you were supposed to have finished the night before.

- You skip class to finish work from another class.

- You often multi-task to get everything done.

- Pulling all-nighters is the norm and you often wonder if you were a vampire in a past life.

Know When You're at Your Best

Before setting out to craft your master schedule, spend a few days keeping track of what you do all day, from the minute you wake up until you sleep. Many students are surprised about the amount of wasted time and how quickly the small breaks add up. You may also gain some other keen insights about yourself and your habits.

- Maybe you start reflecting on that thrilling episode of your favorite show in the afternoon instead of reading the book in front of you. This means afternoon studying sessions will be no good, and should be used for break time.

- Maybe you wonder why you can never get work done in the morning and realize it's because you study in the lounge with all your friends at this time. It might be time to switch it up and go to the library.

- Although you might feel guilty about taking an hour break for dinner with your friends, you see that post-dinner time is when you have the most productive study sessions. Now you can enjoy your time guilt-free.

Fun Fact

In his book, *Daily Rituals: How Artists Work,* Mason Currey details how the most infamous artists and intellectuals spend their time. Charles Dickens went to bed at midnight and wrote every day from nine in the morning to three in the afternoon. Sigmund Freud didn't sleep until one in the morning and worked all throughout the day with one-hour breaks every so often.

Find out when you study the best by making note of the most and least efficient study sessions — which will probably vary on a daily basis. Some students may have two relatively easy morning classes and are able to study mid-morning until their lunch break three days a week. On the other two days, however, they may have two difficult, draining classes in the morning, so mid-morning study sessions wouldn't be productive.

Tip #1

You know yourself better than anyone else does, so set aside study time when you are the most productive. If you're a morning person, study in between morning classes. If you find yourself having more energy at night, set aside an hour or two before dinner.

While this may change from semester to semester depending on your class load and schedule, it's important to note that most successful students are able to work between breakfast and dinner. Students usually socialize after dinner, and even if you have a quiet night, taking a break after dinner allows your body and mind to wind down from the day. Granted, this is not true for everyone, but those who can find time to study before dinner and relax in the evening are rejuvenated and ready when they wake up the next morning.

Basically, heed Plato's advice, and "know thyself" and your habits, your daily and weekly mojo, and then, you can get to work.

Getting to the Craft: Making Your College Schedule

Now that you've evaluated your time-spending habits, you can take a look at the college classes available to you. In college, you'll get to choose what classes to take and there will usually be a large range of class times available to pick from. After doing the aforementioned exercise, you should have a clear idea of when your focus is at its peak and pick classes that take place during these times. Avoid picking solely Tuesday/Thursday classes, which may give you a dreamy four-day weekend, but cause you to be burnt out and lethargic on the days when you don't have anything to do. Again, though, this is up to your discretion, and experiment how you see fit.

When setting to work with your schedule, be it on an online calendar or a day-by-day agenda, be sure to put in any classes, appointments, or any known commitments first. Then start fantasizing about the next Net-flix-binging sessions and pizza nights or extracurricular clubs you'll want to engage in. Even if you're dead-set on having a Friday off or making sure you get three hours a day of relaxation, just make sure to schedule study times when you know you'll be focused.

Fun Fact

Most college extracurricular activities will have their meeting times and locations set before the year, so if you're set on a particular organization or activity, get their info *before* picking your classes.

Which brings us to the next question: "How much time am I going to spend hitting the books?" On average, successful students spend two hours a week studying for every hour per week spent in class. That could be anywhere from 24 to 30 hours a week. Classes that are particularly demanding may require more time, and students who tend to read slowly should add more time as well.

A shiny and wonderful schedule will be made with the following considerations:

- Gaps between classes can be twice as productive as other times. Make sure to leave at least an hour, ideally two or three, between your classes throughout the day.

- Prioritizing times to relax and stay healthy doesn't mean you're lazy. So, don't get over your head and plan a six-hour study block without a time to eat, take a walk, or recharge; it *is* important.

- Being *just* a student who studies and goes to class doesn't mean you're going to succeed. Actively pursue interests outside of college that will give your life meaning and plan accordingly.

- Make a note of your professors' office hours in your agenda. You may need to speak to them.

Commit to Your Learning

Listen, you worked too hard to get to the university. Even if you slacked off in high school, it's a fresh start! Ditch the old, worn-out suit and become the kind of person you may have always dreamed about being: smart, confident, and independent. If you ditched class before, here's your chance: go to class. Dragging your feet because you're too tired and hungry? Dream about your nap after class and bring a protein bar. It's that simple.

Successful students go to class. Many professors admit that unattended classes harm students' grades. Even if the class doesn't have penalties for missing, students suffer solely by not attending and keeping up with class material. Many class periods offer invaluable discussions or information that cannot be replicated by copying someone's notes or reading the textbook. Studies also show that the more people see you on a regular basis, the more they like you! So, let that fresh face of yours be known and earn brownie points with your flawless attendance.

Tip #2

Go to class. There are so many good things that come from interacting face-to-face with your peers and professors. This can range anywhere from becoming more familiar and comfortable with your professors, to meeting friends in your major that last a lifetime, to being able to ask those burning questions in class that come up while you're studying at home.

Here are some other benefits of attending class everyday:

- Being exposed to the subject on a regular basis allows for a more thorough and internalized understanding of it.

- Class participation will get you a little more invested in the learning process. And once you show up, you can always make sure to ask the professor questions once the class lets out.

- Successful students avoid grade penalties from unexcused absences by attending all their classes.

- Showing up sends a strong message: "I'm here and committed to doing the best I can." So, when you're struggling or have a family emergency that requires you to miss class, a professor will be much more understanding because your initiative has already come across with your flawless attendance.

In the Trenches: Strategizing Your Study Blocks

Long blocks of time set aside for studying can seem daunting, if not terrifying. Here are some tips to plan a balanced and successful session:

- *Take breaks.* Studies on productivity show that concentrated activity should last no longer than 50 minutes and there should be 10-minute breaks in between. Go for a walk, have a snack, chat with friends, check your email, or stretch and take a bathroom break.

- *Switch it up.* After the break, successful students change subjects or tasks. Reading the same textbook for hours won't work.

- *Plan ahead.* Successful students bring all supplies and materials needed for the assignment or project. There is nothing worse than getting ready to study then realizing that last week's notes are still at home.

- *Prioritize.* Hard work should be completed at the beginning of your study session when your mind is still fresh.

Think About Exceptions and Make Time for You

No schedule is complete without making room for the unexpected. There might be obstacles thrown at you in your personal life or problems that can't be anticipated that cause you to dramatically rearrange your schedule. These are the times when it feels like nothing's going your way and may even start to pile up. Sometimes the little distractions, such as friends, phone calls, and computer time, take over and you don't even realize it. Either way, they all leave a huge dent in your schedule, and there are some other time-sucking hazards to consider:

- A friend has an emergency and needs help.

- A boss has requested that all employees work more hours during an anticipated busy week.

- A professor announces a change in the syllabus, which adds an assignment or more material to read and study.

- You feel the effects of stress and decide to take a "mental health day." Taking a break is okay once in a while, as long as you know that there will be extra work to catch up on the next day. Sometimes, it's worth it.

You'll groan thinking about how right adults were when they cautioned: "Life gets real, real fast." The days of afternoon television are over, and soon enough, your family may need you, you might take on a job, or you might go through your first big break up. With all these things in mind, it's not hard to get burnt out or start to think negatively about being in school. That's why you should make time for *fun*.

Tip #3

Make time for yourself. It's important to be able to step outside of any worries or frustrations with school and just enjoy doing the things that make you *you*. Watch an episode of your favorite show or go for a long walk on campus listening to music. Get off campus, explore the town, and go to a restaurant with your friends or to your favorite independent bookstore.

Making memories will anchor you when the winds start blowing you off course. You may have to stay up after a shift at work to study for your exam, but at least the day after, you've made plans on going to a concert with some new friends.

Making new friends to spend time with does take initiative in college, but if you start with what *you're* interested in, they'll fall into place. In college, friendships are more defined by your passions, hobbies, and other pursuits. That's why it's important to explore the different clubs and opportunities available to you.

- Join an academic club or organization: Most university departments have discipline-related clubs and organizations. Students can also find honors societies and competition-based teams to join and make connections as well.

- Become a member of a social organization: These are clubs and organizations that aren't necessarily affiliated with a discipline on campus but appeal to leisure activities such as the outdoor club, poetry club, or film society.

- Take advantage of the university's resources: This includes art and history galleries, planetariums, theaters, and volunteer organizations.

- Make use of the student union: Student unions offer a variety of entertainment activities including outside performers (such as speakers, comedians, and musicians) and internal performers, such as students who like to perform.

Students can get more information by reading the university's publications, checking out information boards in the student union, and asking around. Basically, take initiative, look at fliers, and attend whatever event or club that seems the most compelling to you.

Tip #4

Get involved — networking is invaluable in college. You can form friendships, make professional connections, or maybe even meet your future spouse (wink, wink)!

Fun Fact

The founders of Whole Foods and the Container Store, two very successful companies that pride themselves on community-building and fair treatment of their employees and customers, were roommates in college!

On a Steep Climb: Surviving Exam Weeks

Let's say for some obscure reason you're asked to climb up a large, steep mountain. As you walk towards the towering incline after a long hike, you'll want to have been prepared, right? This incline represents your exam weeks, which are arduous journeys indeed. Although doing well on your exams starts from sticking to your schedule throughout the semester, they are stressful even for the most organized students. Here are some quick tips for how to stay sane during this time:

- Stay healthy: It's more important than ever for you to continue exercising and eating right so your body can function with the added stress of late nights and a huge workload.

- Take breaks: It may seem like there's no time for a break with so much work to do, but many successful students have found that when they aren't getting far in their work, it's time to take a break—even if it's for only 10 minutes.

- Work ahead: Having a schedule that clearly illustrates everything that is due on a certain day helps you prioritize and even get some work done early. There is no reason why a project or paper shouldn't be done the week before it's due to make time for studying the following week.

- Commit to your schedule every week: Every time you make your schedule for the week, stick to it. The more you miss, the more this will add up when it's time to study for a big test.

Exercise: Create a Schedule

So, what exactly will you use to plan your time now that you know how? You could use an electronic calendar and sync it up with your phone so that you receive alarms. You could buy a whiteboard calendar for your dorm room. Or, you could stick with an old-fashioned agenda, one that you take with you in your backpack. There are a lot of fun options, but it's ill-advised to use more than one. When you forget what you were supposed to do that day, you'll want to have a time bible, something you *know* will have the information you need. Some students might use a large monthly calendar for holidays or big events, but you'll need a planner that has an hourly breakdown of each day, not just an infinitesimal square where you'll be cramming in all of your to-dos.

The weekly schedule

	Monday	Tuesday	Wednesday	Thursday	Friday	Saturday	Sunday
7.00 am							
7.30 am							
8.00 am							
8.30 am							
9.00 am							
9.30 am							
10.00 am							
10.30 am							
11.00 am							
11.30 am							
12.00 am							
12.30 am							
1.00 pm							
1.30 pm							
2.00 pm							
2.30 pm							
3.00 pm							
3.30 pm							
4.00 pm							
4.30 pm							
5.00 pm							
5.30 pm							
6.00 pm							
6.30 pm							
7.00 pm							
7.30 pm							
8.00 pm							
8.30 pm							
9.00 pm							

Ideally, your schedule is in a week-by-week format, with an hour-by-hour slot available for each day. When filling it out, try using different colored pens for different kinds of activities, which can signal your brain before you even read the text. Within each block, make sure to note the to-dos, important deadlines, tests, and the like. For instance, say you see a huge study block on the day before you have an in-class quiz for Spanish and an assignment due in philosophy. Your block might look like this:

TUESDAY

6	Coffee!! ☕
7	
8	Class
9	
10	
11	
	STUDY BLOCK!
12	
1	Study for Spanish &
2	Finish Philosophy Reflection
3	
4	
5	Class
6	
7	Dinner w/ friends
8	

In this case, you may want to re-write this block onto a post-it for easy reference as you go along. The most important thing is that the student has exemplified everything mentioned in this chapter. The time to study was chosen at a peak focus time; in this case, early afternoon. This slot could be between their morning and afternoon class, thus maximizing in-between times. Each task is broken down so they know exactly what to do and how to do it. In other words, they've mastered the craft of scheduling in a way that keeps them sane, organized, and productive.

Tip #5

Keep an organized schedule. At the beginning of every week, strategize for what you'll need to get done to set yourself up for success for the following ones. Setting aside a few minutes to organize your entire week will save you tons of stress and anxiety.

Chapter 2

Organize Your Life

Even the best time management and study skills can't help college students if their materials are unorganized. In high school, it might have been as simple as two big textbooks, a folder, and a multi-subject notebook. In college, the number of tools necessary for your maintenance will multiply four-fold: you'll receive in class handouts and sometimes lengthy academic articles, need multiple books per course per semester, and will likely have multiple notebooks and assignment folders. Some of us may thrive in the chaos of an unorganized life, but in college, the chaos can escalate more quickly than you may be able to handle.

When in doubt, heed the words of Christina Scalise, an organization guru: "Organization isn't about perfection. It's about efficiency, reducing stress and clutter, saving time and money, and improving your overall quality of life." This chapter will hopefully teach you to do just that.

Organize the Backpack, Papers, and Supplies

Let's start with the backpack. It might have been typical for you to get a new backpack every year—maybe a nice Jansport with one small pocket and a large one. For your freshman year, try one that has multiple pockets. You'll need room for the large textbooks and folders, but also a way of compartmentalizing the tiny essentials. You will have lots of different things you'll need to carry with you, and here are some suggested organization tools to keep your backpack light and well-sorted (instead of a vacuous hole):

- *An accordion-style file organizer:* These aren't just great emulations of a whimsical instrument. They are huge upgrades from the puny file folders you might have gotten in high school that hold more paper, and have tiny tabs where you can write subject names. They're also much larger and more difficult to lose than flimsy one-subject folders, and much more fun to open.

- *Supply wallets:* There are two kinds of students in high school. Those who bring the pencils, and those who don't. For whatever reason, the transition from high school to college also results in a transition from pencils to fine-point pens. Since you'll be doing a lot of writing, most people find it more comfortable to write with a nice, smooth pen instead of a pencil that could break every five minutes. So, buy a pack of 10, and get a supply wallet: some kind of zipper plastic pouch where you can carry them, along with your highlighters, post-its, and other note-taking supplies.

- *Flip-style notebooks:* Why? Because they're fun to flip. And you feel like you're on an episode of "Law and Order." And, as you may have noticed, the older you get, the more your classroom desks tend to shrink. Most college students overlook this fact and go right for that fat three-subject notebook they'd use in high school. Not only are these huge notebooks hard to carry around, but they'll be difficult to write on when you have a very small desk. With a 100-page flip-style notebook for every subject, you'll be able to carry around only what you need, and write your notes with class without steam blowing out of your ears.

- *Emergency kit:* If you want to go above and beyond, make yourself an emergency kit. This could have an unopened case of pens, earbuds for when the library gets noisy for your music, a small pocket dictionary, small snacks, and maybe a couple of bucks if you need some tea or coffee.

Tip #6

Keep school supplies organized and neat. Scattered study guides and torn term papers won't get you very far — not to mention if you neglect to bring a pen or pencil to write notes with.

Now on to the next order of business: papers. The different kinds of papers you get in college could be its own category on *Jeopardy*. Here is a comprehensive list of what papers you'll have to carry around, and how to organize them:

- *Your own assignments:* In college, you will be writing reflections, big papers, final papers, and completing a variety of written exercises. The accordion-style binder should work great for these. When you get a lot of work handed back, don't carry these around in your backpack unless you absolutely need to. Instead, find a place in your desk where you can organize returned work.

- *Syllabi:* In college, the syllabus is your guide to the class, just as this book is a guide to your college experience. It is probably the most important document in the class and losing it could result in a loss of cred with the professor. Either make copies of these guys and post them on your wall, write down every single due date in your agenda, or put them in an accordion-style file organizer.

- *Academic articles:* Lots of college professors like to go green and post the articles or readings on a shared website with students. There will be times, however, when you need to print the physical copy so you can highlight and take notes on the page. In these cases, make sure to *date them,* and organize them from the oldest to most recent for your ease of reference.

Fun Fact

Reading on paper and turning pages of a book activates the spatio-temporal parts of the brain, which helps you remember what you read. Although there are lots of environmental benefits to going digital, some people find reading on-screen difficult, and will sometimes forget the most important parts of the text.

In terms of supplies, this just depends on you. Most of the basics have been covered: tools for organizing your papers, writing utensils, an emergency kit, and flip-style notebooks. But below is a comprehensive list that you can copy down as a checklist, because no good scout goes to camp unprepared:

☐ A week-by-week agenda with an hourly breakdown for each day

☐ A backpack with three or more pockets

☐ Fine point pens

☐ Highlighters

☐ Post-its and page markers

☐ A calculator

☐ An emergency kit

☐ An accordion-style file organizer with six or more sections

☐ A big whiteboard calendar for your dorm room for important dates

Basically, you want anything and everything that will simplify your life. If you don't use post-its and know in your deepest of hearts you never will, don't buy them! If you're not taking a math class in college, why would you buy a calculator? Don't. The only thing you need a definite system for is your papers and you'll need to stick to whatever system you decide on — you don't want to be the nutty student scrambling through your papers only to realize you forgot your midterm paper underneath a pile of crud at home.

Tip #7

Invest in durable folders and notebooks. Your chemistry notes won't do you any good if they become a crumpled, ripped mess.

Dress for Success

There's something satisfying about going out in your pajamas, isn't there? Some students enjoy showing up to their classes and plopping down in the front seat dressed in a full bathrobe like "The Dude" in "The Big Lebowski." It may be comfortable. It may be a statement you're trying to send to our society. Fight it all you want, but the fact is it just doesn't look good, and it won't make you feel good either.

When students wear sweats and other comfortable lounging clothes, they often feel less like studying and more like lounging in the sun. This doesn't mean you have to show up looking like you're at an interview every day, but you should definitely get up and get ready, take a shower, and comb your locks. Most students agree that if they feel good about themselves, they often do better when it comes to school, work, and studying.

Here are a couple of reasons why taking care of your appearance _does_ matter:

- Students who dress for class make a better impression on their professors.

- Students who get dressed tend to be more energetic and willing to get to work done even during "down" time.

- Students who dress for class make a better impression on their classmates and are taken more seriously in study groups and other group activities.

- Human nature shows that people strive to meet expectations set upon them. Students who care about their appearance and strive to make a good impression on others soon find that other people have higher expectations of them. Likewise, lower expectations are set on those who don't show that they care about their appearance.

Tip #8

Get dressed every single day — even on your days off. You'll feel energized and ready to be productive even if you never leave your apartment or dorm room.

Maybe you're one of those people who fight against "appearance centrism" and don't dress up as a way of speaking your mind. But even "The Dude" in "The Big Lebowski" couldn't fight the exciting feeling of wearing a new suit. Just keep in mind, the classroom isn't your living room, and it's not as "laid back" as some of your high school classes might have been. As long as you've taken some time for proper grooming and show up on time, that's enough to start building up a stellar reputation.

Exercise: Make it Work! Organize Your Study Supplies

Successful students aren't afraid to dump their backpack and clean out their mess. Don't wait until you get a new one — do this now. Dump everything out, get rid of trash, and start organizing. Make a list of all the things you need for school and studying and get rid of anything that shouldn't be in there. While you may be tempted to bring a hairbrush, or throw in some random things that shouldn't be there, ask yourself: "Do I want hair on my homework? Do I need to bring my personal diary to class and think about my life while learning about the American Revolution?"

Try compartmentalizing as much as you can. Say you have different supplies for art and math. Get two separate pouches for each subject: one for your calculator, compass, ruler, and another for your colored pencils, charcoal, and other art supplies. If you're reading this and still in high school, go out to an office supply store and experience the magic of an accordion binder. If you have five subjects, make sure to get one with five files, and use color-coded tabs for each. Start using this to organize handouts, assignments, and returned work.

Plant the seeds for a blossoming college career now. Get a system going, and make it work. You might even get some nods of approval from your high school teachers who are used to seeing students in sweats and carrying crumpled papers.

Exercise: Evaluate Appearance and its Effects

There is a plethora of quotes and sayings about taking care of yourself, and giving the world what you want to receive back. They don't need to be said here ad nauseam. Instead, experiment with this kind of thinking in a practical way and take notes. One day, try wearing your most comfortable relaxing clothes and take notes on how you feel. The other, pick out something you know is practical and makes you feel just a little more refined and mature. This could be a button up shirt and a nice pair of jeans, or anything that makes you feel just a little more sophisticated than usual. Take notes, be honest with yourself, and report back to your wardrobe!

Tip #9

Make yourself look presentable even when you think it doesn't matter. You never know who you are going to run into on the way to class or in lecture. It's been proven that dressing nice is linked to a boost in confidence as well. And again, what if you meet your future husband or wife? Do you really want them to see you for the first time dressed in sweats?

Chapter 3

On the Road to Intellectual Enlightenment: Learning Styles and How to Use Them

*E*veryone can admit that our educational system isn't perfect. It has its flaws, areas for improvement, and biases just as people do. This chapter aims to address and alleviate the effects of the system's bias toward "linguistic learning." Basically, education delivered through language and language alone. Think about how much writing, speaking, and listening you have to do on a daily basis in school. Not only are students inundated with writing and reading assignments, but they are also expected to remember class information through linguistic mean, and are not frequently taught individual ways of digesting information.

In this chapter, we'll be introducing a cornucopia of learning styles that may truly enlighten how you think about learning. You might even have a renewed motivation to do well in school after discovering a style that works for you and makes what you learn more engaging. Dare we say, you might even have...*fun?*

Tip #10

Use your time wisely. It's okay to give yourself a break every once in a while, but make sure to dedicate a large portion of your day to focusing yourself on what's important or prioritized in your classes.

Like Uncle Ben reminds Spider-Man, "with great power comes great responsibility." You will find greater degrees of power through freedom in college, but are ultimately *more* responsible and accountable for your learning. You'll have many more choices, and you might find yourself choosing more positive ones simply because you're allowed the freedom to. Although if you want to make the most of your experience, you have to take responsibility by *learning how you learn.*

Fun Fact

Pew Research Center surveyed recent college graduates and asked them if they thought getting their undergraduate degree was "worth it." This could mean in terms of how much they learned and matured from the experience, or in terms of career payoffs and financial gain. Nine in 10 reported that yes, it was worth it.

Activate the Active Learner

Active learners may be the ones listening to facts and statistics and thinking: "So what? How does this apply to me and the world around me?" It's the kind of thinking resonant with Benjamin Franklin's statement on the nature of teaching and learning: "Tell me and I forget. Teach me and I'll remember. Involve me and I learn." The active learner needs to feel like they can use their knowledge for themselves or to an end that reaches beyond the classroom.

Richard M. Felder and Barbara A. Soloman's article defines active learning in more precise terms in "Learning Styles and Strategies." Active learners need to use information at hand to be able to internalize, remember, and understand learning material. They learn most successfully through discussions and practical applications, and struggle in classes that consist primarily of lectures that are devoid of these opportunities. According to Felder and Soloman, active learners need to take the extra initiative to make up for this lack of active learning in order to be successful. Suggestions for this include:

- Organizing a study group

- Explaining concepts to others

- Simulating problem-solving exercises

- Asking the professor for ideas of activities that can help them actively process information

- Seeking out free websites, study aids (such as Smokin' Notes), and learning centers that can help them put information to practical use

- Attending tutoring sessions that allow groups to actively discuss topics with professors or teacher's assistants

Tip #11

Mix up your studying methods. This will allow you to practice recall of information in different ways, aiding in retention.

Activate the Reflective Learner

Are you that person we see in the movies looking soulfully into a clear pond, just pondering your existence and the hidden meanings in your surroundings? Do you learn most when you're not being talked at, when you're just by yourself? If so, you may be a reflective learner.

Reflective learners prefer to think about information before talking about it or putting it to use, preferring solitary learning time. Reflective learners often struggle in fast-paced classes that don't allow time to reflect, such as a wordy or dense lecture, short class discussions, or labs that last an entire class period. At times, it may appear that reflective learners are at a disadvantage, but as Felder and Soloman point out, there are lots of things they can do to feel empowered in their learning:

Tip #12

Contemplate assigned readings before class so you have a basic idea about what will be discussed.

☑ During contemplation, zero in on one or two compelling things in the text. If you're reading about a concept, think about a person in your life or a world event that it relates to.

Tip #13

Think about the material before and after class, ponder on how it applies your experience, knowledge, and the world around you. Make connections; information doesn't have to and shouldn't be detached from who you are. If *you* aren't involved, what's the point?

☑ If you have one really interesting class and one really boring one, try to connect information from the interesting one to the less favored one. Maybe you're learning about the forces behind pollution in a sociology class and can apply this to what you're learning in biology.

Tip #14

Spend time comparing notes taken in class with those from the text, then create your own summary of the information.

☑ A good way to do this is to color code your notes for the lecture and the textbook, using different colors for each, but *using the same color for the same concepts and terms* so you have a benchmark for comparison.

Tip #15

Digest the freshly learned knowledge somewhere calm, quiet, and solitary.

☑ Come up with your own ingenious thoughts: if it's history, think about patterns you see in human behavior. If it's science, think of new solutions to old problems.

Balance Active and Reflective Learning

Do you feel like you walk the line between wanting to apply your knowledge and reflect on it? Felder and Soloman's research states that most students are both active and reflective learners in different scenarios. Students have a strong, moderate, or mild affinity toward one or the other; however, having a solid balance between both is best. Too much active learning can lead to problems in a project or study session, and too much reflective learning can cause students to spend too much time thinking and not enough "doing."

There are ways to achieve this balance:

- Active learners can study with reflective learners, if they are both open to the other's perspective.

- Active learners can purposefully make themselves slow down and think about the topic before jumping right in and doing whatever needs to be done.

- Reflective learners can set aside a time limit for thinking about the topic before they begin their work.

Activate the Sensing Learner

The name sounds a little misleading, but a "sensing learner" is someone who needs to fully make sense of something in practical ways before they learn it. They use their "common" or "practical" sense gained from real world experience to reason their way to a full understanding.

Felder and Soloman state that sensing learners prefer learning facts and solving problems with tried-and-true methods. Sensing learners also memorize and complete lab-type work that has a specific procedure. Overall, sensing learners are practical and need to see how a specific class applies to the real world and struggle in classes if they don't see a clear connection to practical uses.

To expand their learning style, sensing learners should:

Tip #16

Ask the professor for clarifications and connections to real world events.

☑ DON'T ask: "Why should we care?" Rather, frame your question so that it shows you actually do care how the information carries out in reality.

Tip #17

Attend a class discussion group where the members brainstorm real-world connections to help them internalize information.

☑ You don't have to organize this by yourself. Go to your academic organization's center and look into a current events club. In fact, you might have fun creating a legacy for your college by starting your own organization that specializes in knowledge application!

Tip #18

Spend time making connections to your experiences or important memories.

☑ This is best accomplished by promising yourself to incorporate one thing you learned in school in a personal diary entry.

Tip #19

Seek out additional sources that may have more information on how topics apply to current events, other ideas, people, and places.

☑ Since news articles strive to remain objective and detached, this may not be the best choice for a learner who is more interested in consequences. Find a blog where writers talk about their opinions on the future consequences of current events, or use current events to discuss broader issues.

Tip #20

Use examples from the text as a jumping board to reflect and synthesize your observations and life experience with the material.

☑ This may not work for math, but it could work for science, which is ripe with metaphors that relate to how we live our lives.

Activate the Intuitive Learner

Are you more excited to learn in order to experience an "Aha!" moment? Once you learn something, do you start thinking up new, ingenious ideas you swear no one else has thought of? If so, you might be the inspired intuitive learner.

According to Felder and Soloman, intuitive learners absorb information best through discovery, and dislike repetition.

Fun Fact

In his groundbreaking book, *"Wired to Create: Unraveling the Mysteries of the Creative Mind,"* Scott Barry Kaufman says that a variety of experiences, more than anything else, is essential to creativity. If you're an intuitive learner, you may also be a highly creative person, and love to experience new things, shake things up, and avoid anything that makes life more mundane.

Intuitive learners quickly understand new concepts and are often innovative in their studies. Intuitive learners dislike the courses that require memorization and participation in repetitive work.

Intuitive learners are fairly lucky in college because the majority of classes require this type of thinking and application of concepts any way. No generalization comes without its exceptions, though, and intuitive learners may find themselves in classes that require a large amount of memorization and repetitive work. Intuitive learners are often bored and make careless mistakes on exams and assignments because they don't like repetitive questions. Here's what the intuitive learner can do to fight back their tears of boredom in the face of routine:

Tip #21

Pay special attention to the details, especially when completing exams and assignments.

☑ A missed detail could be the difference between an excellent grade and one that's barely passing!

Tip #22

Look up and ask around for professors who don't rely on a ton of memorization in their classes.

☑ You can look for online reviews of their classes (which you should be skeptical of), or ask other students.

Tip #23

Take extra time to think.

☑ Think about different ways the information can be used so you have an idea of what type of purpose it serves while you do repetitive work for class.

Activate the Visual Learner

Felder and Soloman define visual learners as those who need to observe graphics to understand the material —such as pictures, timelines, demonstrations, films, and flow charts. Many might say visual learners have been done a great disservice by the educational system. Contrary to popular belief, it's not as if visual learners are only interested in subjects like art, design, or film. They have a curiosity about the world like anyone else, but simply digest information in a visual way.

Fun Fact

If you're a visual learner and are daunted by the prospects of reading and writing in college, don't feel like you're alone. In fact, it's estimated that 65 percent of the world's population are visual learners, so you're actually in the majority.

As referred to earlier, people who are experts in language tend to excel in school due to the copious amounts of written and verbal educational materials. The visual learner may find themselves struggling, but there are definitely ways they can learn to succeed in college as many of them, in fact, do:

Tip #24

Look up videos, documentaries, or movies that are relevant to what you're learning in class.

☑ Make sure *they actually relate to* the class material. There will be very few instances that a movie like *Mission Impossible* will relate to anything you learn in college.

Tip #25

Take notes in the form of concept maps, graphs, charts, and timelines instead of outlines or lists.

☑ In order to prepare for this, take a little time each day to draw the outlines of your maps before class.

Tip #26

Use colored pens and highlighters.

☑ Color-code your notes to make them more visually appealing. The change in visual cues will likely grab your attention.

Tip #27

You can also organize information by color and create a color key.

☑ There are a variety of ways you could do this (at least as many as there are in the rainbow!). Red could mean questions, blue could mean ideas for a paper, green could be commentary about the reading, and so on and so forth.

Tip #28

Keep the textbook handy during lecture so you can look at graphics while the professor discusses the topic.

☑ Make sure it doesn't look like you're catching up on reading in class by making frequent eye contact and looking from the textbook to what's on the board.

Activate the Verbal Learner

If you're a verbal learner, you have certainly hit the jackpot when it comes to academia, and you won't be the one with the sweaty brow when you see a ton of readings on the syllabus. Verbal learners command language with ease and access knowledge through spoken and written words. Although verbal learners may find themselves kicking back with a tropical drink in their college classes, they can still learn more skills to improve their learning style.

Tip #29

Participate in study groups that discuss and explain the topics.

☑ Again, you don't have to create these groups on your own. Ask around and you may find one that already exists.

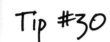

Use mnemonics to remember facts.

☑ Believe it or not, they do work!

Create rhymes and rhythms to remember facts and concepts.

☑ Rhymes may actually help you remember more. Why else would those old commercial jingles be riddled with rhymes?

Write and rewrite notes.

☑ The key is writing your notes in a conversational manner.

Recite information aloud.

☑ Make sure you're in a private place!

Activate the Sequential Learner

When sequential learners process information, it's as if they're building a staircase—they have to build the first step before they jump to the next. Felder and Soloman explain that sequential learners figure out concepts in a logical, step-by-step fashion. They're often referred to as "logical learners," leaning toward subjects like math, philosophy, linguistics, and science. They might get frustrated when confronted with the "scatter-brained professor" who jumps back and forth between topics instead of explaining things in a linear fashion. Coming back to the staircase metaphor, if a logical step is excluded from class, they may need to ask the professor to fill this in.

Tip #34

Spend time after each class re-organizing notes into logical and sequential lists.

☑ Or better yet, try and do this during lecture to the best of your ability to save time.

Tip #35

Discuss the missing areas of information.

☑ Clarify facts with like-minded students in class.

Tip #36

Refer to the textbook.

☑ The textbook can help you visualize a logical framework for the information.

Activate the Global Learner

Some painters start with a tiny detail and paint the rest of the picture from that starting point. Others sketch the whole landscape, needing to see a whole picture before beginning to zoom in and get to work. This is an accurate metaphor for the global learner: they need to understand broader generalizations before they begin internalizing bits of information. The global learner will do well in college if they emulate a hawk, scanning the landscape before swooping in for the kill. Here are some suggested approaches to learning class material:

Tip #37

Skim a chapter before fully reading it.

☑ This way, you can anticipate what is coming up next and get a broad idea of what will be talked about.

Tip #38

Pay attention to the syllabus.

☑ This way, instead of going through the forest of the class step by step, you can get a bird's eye view of the forest, seeing how all of the course content fits together.

Tip #39

Write down the thought processes that led up to figuring out how something worked.

☑ This can be challenging for the global learner who generally doesn't see things through a magnifying glass, so be patient, but know that it's sometimes crucial to understanding the steps in a process.

Tip #40

Pair up with sequential learners.

☑ Students who learn in a linear fashion can help the global learner see how all the details contribute to the solution instead of just looking at the big picture.

What You Can Do Out of Class

Remember, don't get discouraged if you get to lecture and find the professor's teaching doesn't match up with how you learn. If you find a way to make the class important to you, you'll find a way to get through it. For instance, say you're taking a sociology class with a professor who doesn't use graphics and explains things in a chaotic and disorderly way. Beyond their teaching style, they could be talking about some important stuff, like what contributes to global poverty or economic depressions. Isn't that important for you to know as someone who will be out making a career for yourself one day? Isn't it valuable to understand how the world economy works and affects our lives? Remember when you're tempted to blow off the class because it's frustrating to understand: "if there is a will, there is a way," and in order to find a way, you need to find the will first.

Fun Fact

The full quote is from Pauline Kael, one of the most influential film critics in American history: "Where there is a will, there is a way. If there is a chance in a million that you can do something, anything, to keep what you want from ending, do it. Pry the door open or, if need be, wedge your foot in that door and keep it open."

The best advice in these cases is to just take what you can from lectures, and cater the material to your learning style while you study. Remember, you'll be studying for class three times as much as you'll be in it. In the example mentioned, you might read the chapters your professor was lecturing on a second time, and if you're a visual learner, make charts combining chapter and lecture notes. If you're a sequential learner, try organizing the logical steps and asking your professor about the missing gaps. If you're a global learner, try finding hunches for the theoretical framework tying the whole lesson together.

Basically, a professor who isn't an "all-star lecturer" or teaches in a way that doesn't mix well with your learning methods isn't the end of the world. Treat it as an opportunity or challenge that you will ultimately benefit from.

Tip #41

Take the learning style quiz on the following pages to better gauge which style of learner you are.

Which Learning Style Activates You?

Take a look at this guide to learning styles and highlight bullet points that apply to you. Count them up for each section.

Learning Style A	Learning Style B
• Prefer classes that involve memorization and other information. • Need to know how the information/topics/concepts apply to the practical world to fully understand its importance.	• Learn better with visual depictions of the information such as a timeline, chart, graph, or demonstration. • Struggle in classes where the information is provided through lecture with minimal use of visual aids.

Learning Style C	Learning Style D
• Can see the whole picture but often the details are fuzzy. • Know the answer or solution to a problem but often cannot explain the steps to reach that solution. • Need to be able to see the big picture before thinking about how the details fit together.	• Can easily express ideas through writing and speaking. • Prefer lectures versus demonstrations and labs. • Enjoy working with study groups that focus on discussing the information.

Learning Style E	Learning Style F
• Need to use the information to understand it. • Like to discuss information with teachers and classmates. • Prefer labs, practical application, and discussions versus lectures.	• Prefer to use formulas to find answers and understand concepts. • Use lists and other step-by-step formulas for studying and understanding the material.

Learning Style G	Learning Style H
• Need time to think about information before discussing or applying it. • Prefer studying alone versus studying with a group. • Dislike participating in class discussions if there's no time to digest the information first.	• Dislike classes that require memorization and other information. • Become bored with classes that require the repetitive use of concepts and formulas. • Prefer to learn through discovery instead of receiving information upfront.

Key: A = Sensing, B = Visual, C = Global, D = Verbal, E = Active, F = Sequential, G = Reflective, H = Intuitive.

List up to four preferred learning styles below (if you have more than four highlighted in the chart, try to narrow it down to your top four).

1. _____

2. _____

3. _____

4. _____

Part II: Getting Down to Business: What to Do Every Day

Let's say that the first part of the book was preparing for your role as a healthy, well-rounded, and awesome college student whom everyone admires. You've got the costume. You've got the script. You've got the props. Now it's time to actually play the part. Now that we've covered the essentials: organization, scheduling, and learning styles, all the things you can start to develop at any time, we can move on to the college-specific approaches to lengthy reading assignments, lectures, and the kind of critical thinking that will be required of you.

Chapter 4

Letting the Words Sink in and Reading to Know

Maybe in high school you could get away with never even glancing at your textbook. Or, maybe you did read it, and didn't remember a thing. Maybe you read *and* remembered! Either way, reading is a completely different beast in college and it will be the backbone of you learning pretty much everything that is *absolutely necessary*. You'll be pleased to find that there's a greater variety in the readings, which will be much more interesting, clear, up-to-date with exciting new research, and written by people who are passionate about what they do. But they will be *much longer*, and this chapter will help you develop strategies that will allow you to enjoy, take notes on, and fully understand what you read.

Make Reading a Hobby

Fun Fact

A 2013 survey by the Book Trust reported that people who read are, on average, "more satisfied with life, happier, and more likely to feel the things they do in life are worthwhile." There are even "bibliotherapists," professionals who help people find meaning in their lives through books.

Make reading a hobby and you'll only be rewarded for it. Ever find that when someone refers to something they read in a book, they seem inherently more interesting? Quoting something you read on your own that applies to what you're learning in class will do nothing but impress your professor and peers. In fact, you may find that what you've read contradicts what the textbook says, and bringing it up in class can inspire an enlivened discussion that your professors *live for*.

You might say, "How do you expect me to read extra with all these required readings in college?" After college, there will be less and less time to read for enjoyment, and so it's good to develop a habit now and make it count. It's a way of getting you out of your "student bubble" and pursuing your own interests *while* making you a better student. It's a win-win, so why not?

Like a Hawk: Landscaping the Readings

The best way to read in college is to "landscape" the reading first. This basically requires thinking about the reading in a variety of ways before reading it, so you can understand more as you go along, and evaluating how long the reading will take.

Tip #42

Look at how long the chapter is, and break it up logically.

☑ If a chapter is 40 pages long with eight sections, you might try and read two sections at a time. More than page numbers, you're looking at beginning and stopping points that come full circle. In history books, this may be the beginning to the end of a war, historical period, etc.

Tip #43

Skim and read the introduction, summaries, and conclusion.

☑ This will give you a "wide net" that you can use to capture information from that text that ties in with the author's claim and closing remarks.

Tip #44

Think about what you are going to read before you read it.

☑ Look at the titles, pictures, and headings. Think about what you may already know about the subject and what the professor may have highlighted in class.

During this process, you may notice certain organizational patterns that crop up. Academic articles, which you'll be reading *a lot of*, don't have too many headings or subheadings, with most sections lasting at least three to six pages. You will notice, though, that every article will have a "thesis" or claim that they're trying to make. Once you identify this claim, organize your own notes around it while you read.

Focus on the Ideas

This ties into the next point. Sometimes specific details in a text could distract us from the main idea. Maybe the author cites a study on how people who are similar to one another like each other more, and you want to read more on that because it's fascinating. Fascinating or not, the author is using the study to service the whole picture, which is the claim they're trying to make. In this case, you would want to explain in your notes how the study relates to the argument, instead of writing down facts about the study alone. Here are some other ways you can stay on track:

- Only writing one phrase or idea per paragraph

- Reading several paragraphs before writing anything down

- Reviewing and revising notes that contain keywords while thinking or reciting the facts

- Using concept maps or other visual guides to connect ideas

- Reading the conclusion to see how the author connects and applies the ideas in the reading

Master the Art of Skimming

Believe it or not, there is a time and a place for skimming in college. Your high school teachers may have nodded in disapproval when they saw you flip through 20 pages in a minute, but in college skimming is an art that, when perfected, will serve you well. Of course, it should never *replace* reading the text, but here are some scenarios in which skimming is highly encouraged:

Tip #45

Skim the text before and after.

☑ Skimming before allows you to guess at what the author's big picture is.

☑ Skimming after may allow you to fill in important information in your notes or review the reading before an important discussion.

Tip #46

Skim after you read your notes.

☑ If your notes are unorganized or illegible, you may want to just toss them and do them over.

☑ Start skimming each section and filling in the important points in an organized manner on fresh note paper.

☑ Rewriting your notes and skimming is also a great way to review for in-class discussions and tests.

Wake Up from the Snooze with Alarm Words

Stop snoozing and pay attention to the alarm words that the author has kindly written to signal important points in the text. Walter Pauk illustrates these words in his book, *How to Study in College*. Here are some of the examples:

- Words that indicate examples are "specifically," "for example," "for instance," and "to illustrate." These words are clues that you should understand before deciphering the example.

- Words that indicate cause-and-effect are "consequently," "as a result," "accordingly," and "hence." Understanding causation is a huge part of critical thinking, so pay attention to any and all examples of cause and effect in the text.

- Words that indicate enumeration — "first," "second," and "third" — tell you to make sure you understand all the steps in the process being illustrated.

- Words that indicate contrast such as "on the other hand," "however," and "despite," tell you to make sure you understand both sides of the issue. This might be the author's "counterargument" which you may be asked about in class.

- Words that indicate comparisons are "likewise," "similarly," and "identical." These words tell you that two things are similar.

Involve Yourself or What's the Point?

In an earlier discussion in this book, we posed the question: "If *you* are not a part of your learning, if *you* don't take responsibility for your knowledge, then what's the point?" This should be a question that follows you around in college like a fruit fly, pestering you until you're reminded of the answer that you, and you alone, will know. In fact, you should ask yourself this question every time you complete a reading, and take time to reflect on your own thoughts about the text and what *you* want to learn from it. Here are some points for reflection for an array of subjects that you can ponder on after reading:

Tip #47

Reflect on history.

☑ What are some of the common patterns you see in history? Are there similar things happening today? What did people do in history that you think is right or wrong? Do you know people in your life who remind you of certain historical figures?

Tip #48

Reflect on English.

☑ Are there conflicts a character faces that remind you of your own? How does this book compare with some of your favorites? Can you identify why you liked or disliked certain aspects of the book and write them down in a clear and comprehensive way? What writing styles do you like? Try emulating a writing style in your own diary and develop your voice on paper.

Tip #49

Reflect on foreign language.

☑ Try labeling all your favorite things in the language you're learning. Make sure that everything you like to talk about in your first language can be translated into the language you're trying to learn. This is how you can "build an identity" in that language and feel more compelled to actually *learn it.*

Tip #50

Reflect on science.

☑ Think about how what you learn in science can illuminate the world around you. What are some important scientific developments that you care about? How do you see science developing in good and bad ways?

Tip #51

Reflect on social sciences.

☑ Try to think of where you've observed a particular social pattern. How is "the looking glass self" a part of your identity? When was the last time you had two contradicting beliefs and experienced "psychological dissonance?"

Love the Book: Making Notes in Your Textbook

The students who do well care about the material they read and study. When they get the most out of reading or studying, they love the material and start to make the book their own. They can do this by using their own system of notations, marking certain pages, and adding sheets of notes and questions in pages they want to explore more. Any student who has seen books loved by professors has noticed questions, markings, and added notes and can see the book has been referred to numerous times.

Defy conventional wisdom that says: "Writing in the book is abuse!" In college, it is a sign of love, engagement, and a rigorous work ethic.

Some people like to buy used books because they can see what others thought about while reading the book. You get a glimpse of what the reader's life was like by reading what he or she marked and notated, and it may help you in class.

Tip #52

Students who have mastered the art of notating will use different colored pens and highlighters, sticky notes, and note paper. Sticky notes are useful to mark important pages because they can stick out of the book without falling out. Use different colored sticky notes for different themes. Usually, a professor will only ask you to focus on two or three a week.

After the student makeover, your book should possess the following qualities:

- Loose spines

- Colorful pages

- Fanning the book causes pages of handwritten notes to fall out

- Sticky notes decorate the edges of the pages

- Questions, answers, and comments fill the margins

- Diagrams and sketches of graphs, charts, and concept maps appear in blank spaces

Read First, Notate Later

While it's still advised to involve yourself in your learning by making the book your own, don't get too crazy with all the colored pens and sticky notes to the point that you may have a very glamorous but illegible textbook laying in front of you. Definitely use your highlighter, but if you're highlighting the entire page, then you have a problem. This can be easily alleviated by *reading the page first* and then going back with your highlighter and sticky notes.

Tip #53

It is important for students to read a paragraph or a section and then go back and highlight, question, mark, and think about the material. Just like skimming, taking notes is an art that needs to be practiced by:

- Stopping after every paragraph or section and going back to question, comment on, and synthesize the reading

- Making notes on the main points of the text

- Only highlighting main points and phrases

- Writing meaningful comments in the margins that you might use in a class discussion, assignment, conversation with the professor, or exam

- Using the margins to indicate which areas need further research or explanations

Copy onto Paper

Think of notating the book as a preparation for the notes you'll be copying onto paper. Your written notes should be prefaced with an introduction to the text, which should be a summary of what the reading was about (in *your words*). Then, as you copy down the important points you've noted in the book, make sure to include the section titles so that your notes aren't a humongous block of text. Basically, find a way to organize the information in a way that will make sense to you later. As you go along, you can also include your own thoughts that could help you in class or on an assignment. Here are some things to keep in mind when copying the information from the text onto notes:

Tip #54

The best way to learn is through trial and error.

☑ Try out organizational methods until you find one that works for you.

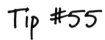

Tip #55

Copying your notes is a great way to study.

☑ That is, if you're copying them down thoughtfully. Take time with them, and you might learn something really valuable.

Tip #56

Make sure to find a way to signify what *kind* of note you're making.

☑ It's easy to get overwhelmed with the amount of notes you have to take. Picking, choosing, and *sorting* is key.

☑ You can sort your notes with symbols or colors that signify the type of note you're making. If it's a question, maybe draw a fat question mark as the bullet point. If it's a personal thought or revelation, make the bullet point a certain color.

☑ Basically, make reference points: you'll be surprised at how little you may remember when looking at your notes later on.

Fun Fact

There are studies that show taking notes may actually make you *forget everything!* When you take notes, the brain basically takes note that the information is already documented, and doesn't move a muscle to remember it! The best way to counteract this is, as suggested, to think critically about the information instead of copying things down word for word.

When It's Time to Make Hard Choices

There will always be days, weeks, or semesters when even the most successful student cannot keep up with all the reading for every class. When this happens, it is time to make hard decisions. Before you start hyperventilating, just know that it will be okay, and there is still hope for you to ace the class as long as you keep your priorities straight:

Tip #57

Find out which sources are most favored by the professor.

☑ Doing this is as simple as looking through the syllabus to see which sources appear most often. These sources should always be read.

Tip #58

Recognize how the professor refers to the reading material in class.

☑ If the professor goes over the reading material specifically, the reading can be skimmed or skipped in these classes if there is a time crunch. *You should always prioritize getting your reading done, as this is the backbone of your education.* Skimming is for emergency use only.

Tip #59

Skim supplementary materials (or skip them) unless the information will appear on the exam.

☑ When it comes down to it, they *are* supplementary. You might find that you find more interesting sources on the subject outside of class anyways.

Tip #60

Evaluate if you need to drop a class and take it at a later time.

☑ Once in a while, students will end up with classes that are all extremely intensive in terms of required reading and they may be better off taking these classes in different semesters.

☑ If this is the case, students can drop a class to take later in their college career.

NOTE: Dropping classes should not become a habit or a crutch for not wanting to examine reading strategies and time management skills. It is also likely that your school has a policy on the number of classes you are allowed to drop. It is important to make several considerations before dropping a class, such as: Is it too late to drop without getting an incomplete? Will dropping the class put the student below a full-time status, and if so, what are the consequences of this? Will there be a charge for dropping the class after a certain date? Is the class a prerequisite for classes that the student plans on taking the following semester?

Get More Out of Lectures

When high school students hear that they'll be going to "lecture" they might think of those intimidating halls with hundreds of seats and one well-dressed professor pacing back and forth, talking for hours on end, while students snore in the back rows. *Real-life lectures aren't like this.* Although it's easy to get stressed, and there are many obstacles you'll have to face in college, lecture is the one time where you can push these worries out of your mind and *be in the present moment with full attention to what's being said.* The professor will often be incredibly passionate, experienced, and excited to be there with a room of hungry minds. So, do them, and yourself, a favor by reading this chapter and learning how to make the most of the class period.

Read the Chapter Before the Lecture

Professors may roll their eyes if you don't do the reading that's on the syllabus on the day it's due. It's not "optional," and it's not something you can just Google; the readings are *mandatory.*

Tip #61

Read before class.

Here are some benefits of doing so:

- Students who make this process a habit prevent themselves from getting behind in the reading and cramming before exams and quizzes.

- Students who do the reading before the class are prepared for surprise quizzes or activities that the professor may decide to do in class.

- Students have a background of the information about which the professor is lecturing. They know the vocabulary—or are at least familiar with it. They also have an idea of what the main points of the lecture may be so they can anticipate what they will be listening to.

Ask One Question During Each Class Period

You're not an empty bucket passively waiting for knowledge to be poured forth onto you. Studies show when you actively engage in class, you tend to like what you learn more.

Tip #62

Ask at least one question during the class period.

This may be a little nerve-wracking at first, but as long as the questions are meaningful and related to the topic, the professors will grace you with a beaming smile. There are many reasons why this is a great idea:

- Asking meaningful questions shows the professor that you're interested in the topic and listening to the lecture.

- Professors will get to know the students who are more vocal in class better than the ones who do not ask questions or participate in discussions.

- Knowing you have to ask one question during each class period will make you pay more attention to what the professor is saying.

- Usually, professors will leave time for questions at the end of the class or at certain points during the class. To avoid interrupting the professor, jot down your questions in context of your notes so you don't forget what you want to ask.

Take Good Notes During Lectures

While taking good notes should never replace listening and actively thinking about what's being said, you should at least take down the notes that you *know are important*. Lectures cannot be repeated, and balancing attentive listening and note taking is no easy task, but here are some tips to help:

Tip #63

Listen for signal words and phrases: "This is important." "This will be on the test." "There are three (or however many) main points . . ."

☑ When you hear those key phrases, bust out your pen and write at lightning speed.

Tip #64

Find a note-taking method that works.

☑ Some students prefer to outline what the professor is saying. This means categorizing information as much as possible, using lots of headings and bullet points.

☑ Others like to make simple lists and organize later, and still others like to make charts and concept maps.

Tip #65

Sit near the front of the class to force yourself to pay attention.

☑ As we'll begin to discuss in a minute, it's always a good idea to sit in front. This way, you feel like the professor is talking *with you* and not *at you*. You'll feel a little more obligated to listen and thus retain information if you're right in front.

Tip #66

Take note of where you think you may have missed something important, and try to fill it in later.

☑ Write some kind of signal phrase, a question mark, and a blank space to fill in the information once you've talked to your professor or a fellow student.

Tip #67

It is OK to stay after class and ask for clarification as long as it is a direct question about a specific part of the lecture.

☑ For example, "I think I missed the third step in the writing process, could you explain it again?" is much better than saying, "I need you to go over the writing process. I think I missed something." Students who have a specific question about a part of the lecture show that they were listening and paying attention. A very general question could end up irritating the professor.

Combine Textbook and Lecture Notes

Tip #68

Master the art of the textbook and lecture notes combo.

Your professor will rarely ever lean on one or the other, and he or she will expect you to synthesize both of them for your assignments and exams.

Here are some pretty effective ways of doing this:

- Method #1: Make a three-column sheet. In the first column, write the keyword or concept. In the second column, reiterate what the text says about it. In the third column, add in what the professor said about it during the lecture.

- Method #2: Combine the ideas in an outline format, paying special attention to repeat material. Material that is in both the textbook and lecture will likely be on exams.

- Method #3: Review and reflect on the material. Review both sets of notes, and reflect on the main ideas.

- Method #4: Summarize the discussed topic. Students who actively read and listen to the lecture are able to summarize the material shortly after the lecture and use the summary to recall the information when they are reviewing for exams.

Beat the Lecture Blues

There are students who use lecture for naptime. The professor will inevitably see them and react in horror and probably think to themselves: "Is this preschool?" Listen, maybe you didn't get the all-star lecturer, maybe you got the one who's a little timid or scattered. Either way, they know some pretty fascinating stuff, and you should do them the respect of showing up at your best:

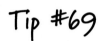

Tip #69

Show up on time and sit near the front.

☑ No, you don't have to stick your head out and validate the professor with a huge smile or anything. Just sit near the front so you can listen with eyes and ears.

Tip #70

Eat a sandwich, and don't starve yourself!

☑ A happy stomach means a happy mind. In fact, if you want to have any ability to focus and really learn, you'll take care of your nutrition. Show up to the lecture after you've had something to eat.

Fun Fact

When thinking of what snacks you should buy, consider walnuts and kiwis, which are super rich in Omega-3s. UCLA researcher Fernando Gómez-Pinilla says: "Omega-3 fatty acids support synaptic plasticity and seem to positively affect the expression of several molecules related to learning and memory ... Omega-3 fatty acids are essential for normal brain function."

Tip #71

Pick lecture times where you're at your peak.

☑ Gone are the days of waking up at 8 a.m. every single day! Yay! Now that you can pick your schedule, pick lectures when you know you'll be able to focus.

Tip #72

Know the professor, and be kind, courteous, and proactive in his or her presence.

☑ This doesn't mean you have to raise your hand every five minutes in class. You don't really want to come off as "needy" or desperate for validation from the teacher. When dealing with the professor, it's essential to have tact: if you see them having a long conversation after class, email them with your question. Go to their office hours *prepared with questions you really want answered.* Don't just go for brownie points. Go because you really want to learn.

Tip #73

Be interested, but know your boundaries.

☑ College can be a difficult time, and it might be tempting to try and ask for personal advice from your professor. In most cases, they'd react kindly, but just know it's not really appropriate. Instead, you might ask them about their research, advice on how to be a better student, or talk about things going on in the department.

Exercise: Try Out Different Note-Taking Strategies

Go to lecture one day with your hand ready for speed. Try to write down almost everything that the professor said and after lecture, write a paragraph about what your experience was.

Now, go to lecture and ***don't take any notes at all***. Make sure you actively listen and ask questions, and write down your notes after class. Write a paragraph comparing this to taking incredibly detailed notes.

Now try balancing the two methods. Pick whichever one helps you remember the most and allows you to enjoy the lecture to the fullest.

The Power of Critical Thinking

A lot of high school students who are honest with themselves will admit that they didn't learn how to think critically, or they didn't have to apply it that much. Maybe you skated by, comfortable with what you know, but not challenged to go the extra mile and really *think* about what you know. Should we just assume that we're better people because of science, as the textbook tells us, or are there ways in which we've become worse? The sky is blue, sure, but why is it blue?

For students who have never thought critically about class material, the process can be overwhelming and frightening because many students do not know what it is or how to do it. Critical thinking is not a natural ability but with a few key tips and tricks, students can train their brains to critically analyze information.

Sometimes called evaluative thinking, critical thinking refers to evaluating the material at hand. Successful students who think critically about the information presented to them do not just accept a claim as is or assume it's right. They question it, and try to take it one step further. This means they try to apply it, think about if it's based on valid points, or disprove it for the sake of understanding it better.

Your college professors will ask you to become a critical thinker, regardless of what you study, because it's the bedrock of learning. What we've covered so far in terms of time management, organization, learning styles, and note-taking are all great tools. But when you sit down and write your papers, you'll be using one thing: your ability to critically analyze.

Understand the Importance of Lateral Thinking

Edward de Bono, an expert on thinking, defines two different types of critical thinking: lateral thinking and vertical thinking. Lateral thinking is the type of thinking that aims to broaden the knowledge base through the generation of new possibilities. Successful students use lateral thinking strategies to help them find new information as well as to examine new perspectives.

Here's how successful students expand their lateral thinking skills:

- *They read a lot.* They read their course material, the newspaper, fiction, non-fiction, magazines, and whatever they can find. Reading about other people's experiences, thoughts, and opinions helps the successful student have a myriad of information from which to draw new ideas and possibilities when they are trying to broaden their knowledge about a topic.

- *They feed their curiosity.* Instead of skimming over information or telling themselves they will find out more later, they take the time to find the answers to their questions when they are reading their texts for class or when they are reading for pleasure.

- *They keep running lists of questions that pop up in their head in a journal or elsewhere so they can go back and answer them when they have time.* When students take a genuine interest in the world around them and unlock their curiosity, they find they have many questions waiting to be answered.

- *They are not afraid to ask new questions and try new things*, such as listening to a speaker with a differing viewpoint, or one with whose topic they are not familiar, or by trying an activity they have never done. New activities can change the way successful students think about familiar experiences and ideas, as well as help them broaden their thinking when they encounter new ideas.

Understand the Importance of Vertical Thinking

Vertical thinking is the thinking system that makes judgments on current information. It's sort of the "aftermath" of lateral thinking. Vertical thinking is developed after you have considered all possible viewpoints, possibilities, and connections, and it begins when you start selecting the most valid ones.

Tip #74

Try out a wide range of ways to flex your vertical thinking muscle.

Experiment with each of the following to see which one fits you best:

- Listing the pros and cons of each possibility

- Looking for other viewpoints during this evaluation process whether it is from friends, classmates, or professors

- Thinking about the realities of each possibility before picking the most valid one

- Breaking the claims down individually and identifying which ones are true

- Weighing in with opposing viewpoints

Balance Lateral and Vertical Thinking

Tip #75

Use lateral thinking first to generate a list of possible solutions to a problem, and then move to vertical thinking to evaluate and choose the best possibility.

It might actually be difficult to understand the two in isolation because they go together like peanut butter and jelly. How could you ever separate them? Be mindful of the following ways these two thought processes can work together:

- When deciding on a topic for a paper or presentation, successful students use lateral thinking to come up with a list of possible topics that fit in the assignment's parameters and then use vertical thinking to narrow it down to the best possible topic for them.

- When answering a short answer or essay prompt on an exam, successful students take a few minutes to think about all the possible directions they may take with the answer and then use vertical thinking to narrow it down to the best possibility.

Be Aware of Assumptions

Tip #76

Never make assumptions. Ever.

Everyone functions on a daily basis as a result of assumptions. This includes the unsaid, second-nature assumptions about manners, daily routines, or social etiquette. Students also make assumptions about what will be covered on an exam, what the professor is saying, and what we learn.

The first types of assumptions are harmless and necessary to function in life. The second type of assumptions may be better off examined. Successful students, for example, know that it is better to think critically about what the professor may include on the exam, instead of assuming it will only be information from the lecture or from the book and then find out they are grossly unprepared for the exam.

Assumptions are your No. 1 enemy in college. Breaking them down is the first step in your career as a mindful, critical thinker. Before you even begin the process of making a claim, you have to make sure all of the evidence you're basing it on is true, and that you're *not assuming anything.* Here are some ways to help overcome common assumptions:

- Successful students do not assume they know everything about a subject, even if they took the same one in high school. Our best advice: having the attitude of "I know nothing and have everything to learn" is *actually a lot smarter and more respected* than "I know everything, look at how much I know!"

- Successful students take the time to fully understand the complexity and workload required for assignments before writing them off as easy or quick projects. This allows them to schedule ample time to complete the project. They do not assume it will be a quick project based on their first glance.

- Successful students utilize their professor's office hours by going in for clarifications on class information as well as assignment directions instead of guessing or assuming they know what the professor means. You don't look ignorant for taking charge of your learning and making sure you're setting yourself up for success.

Exercises in Critical Thinking

Successful students who understand the concepts of critical thinking take their studying a step further than those who do not understand the importance of critical thinking. Here are some exercises to practice that will take you that extra step further:

- Take the time to find practical applications for the material, and figure out how the same ideas can be applied to different situations, as well as the ramifications of doing so.

- Take advantage of assignments by thinking about the posed problems and the possible solutions before answering with the first thought that comes to mind. Evaluate possible solutions and figure out which one is the best fit.

- Practice lateral thinking, vertical thinking, and breaking down assumptions on a regular basis until it becomes a normal part of your day. After consciously doing these things, you will think critically about everything as if it was second nature.

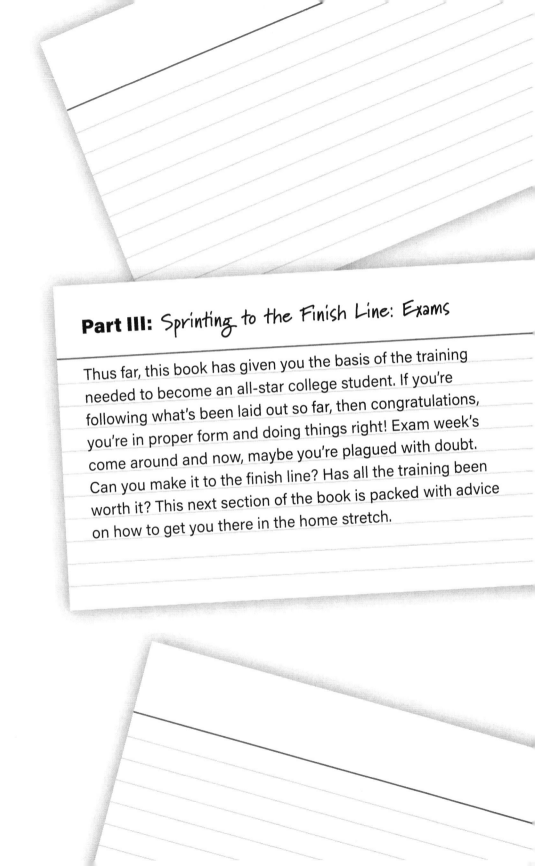

Part III: Sprinting to the Finish Line: Exams

Thus far, this book has given you the basis of the training needed to become an all-star college student. If you're following what's been laid out so far, then congratulations, you're in proper form and doing things right! Exam week's come around and now, maybe you're plagued with doubt. Can you make it to the finish line? Has all the training been worth it? This next section of the book is packed with advice on how to get you there in the home stretch.

Chapter 7

Knowing When to Prepare

Don't worry, it's not like your professors live for exam weeks to torture you or want to make the tests exceptionally difficult. They just want to know that you're learning and progressing in your knowledge about the subject. In reality, if you've been practicing good habits like we've laid out in the first six chapters, your study sessions for midterms and final exams *might only be reviewing and practicing for an in-class essay.* The metaphor for exams as a race to the finish is perfect, because if you've been slacking off most of the time, your tests will be like trying to sprint in a marathon.

There is a time, though, to start preparing specifically for exams and it's advised to *start early.*

Allot Enough Time and Start Early

The general agreement is students should allot eight to 10 hours of study time for each test. Ten hours sounds like a massive block of time for studying, especially for students who study on a whim for an hour or two the night before a test. Here's the thing. That may work to just barely pass a test in high school, but it will have you landing flat on your face in college. When you study for your midterms, you're also studying for your finals, which could be a month or two away.

Tip #77

Stop procrastinating, once and for all.

Before you roll your head back and say to yourself: "They tell me to stop procrastinating every time. They don't get it. I'm an expert at getting my work done the night before; I rock it. I also have better things to do than homework," think about this: you're in college for a reason. You won't *really* get a do-over. If your purpose is to do lazy, last-minute work *and not even enjoy what you're learning*, why are you there?

Here are some reasons to stop the procrastinating and consider starting fresh and early:

- You're more likely to enjoy what you're learning. When you give yourself space to breathe, you might find yourself incredibly motivated to internalize the material so you can use it later on.

- You can motivate your friends in class to start early too. That way, you can have invigorating and interesting talks with your friends and learn the material while having some fun.

- Yikes! What if you're missing notes? What if you realized you missed a lecture? Well, it's a good thing you started early! Now you can ask your professor or a friend to help you fill in the missing information. Or, would you prefer this to be a mystery to solve the day of your exam?

Dig It Up And Break It Up

A good way to start is to figure out as much information as possible about the test. In other words, dig! Investigate! Be a detective and ask the professor and students who have previously taken the class questions about the exams. This isn't cheating—it's preparation. There are two important types of questions student detectives should ask when preparing for exams: questions about format and questions about content.

Questions to ask about the format:

- How many questions will be on the exam?

- What type of questions will be on the exam (essay, multiple choice, true or false, and so forth)?

- How much time will there be to complete the exam?

- Where will the testing room be? In large classes, the students may be separated into several rooms for the exam.

- Will the students be required to answer all the questions or will there be a choice of answering only a certain number of questions?

Questions to ask about the content:

- What material will be covered on the exam?

- Is there a study guide for the exam?

- Will the professor conduct a study session for the exam?

- Are there one or two specific parts of the information that are more important to focus on?

- What supporting materials will be covered on the exam?

Once you have enough information, you can get to work.

Tip #78

Start planning a study schedule four or five days before the day of the exam.

The first study session should be spent organizing the materials and the next three or four sessions should be studying the materials using a variety of study methods.

No, studying isn't just sitting at a 90-degree angle and digesting information as if you were eating a huge meal. It's much more active than that, if you're doing it right. It takes preparation, organization, and focus. Here are some things to consider as you study for your next big exam:

- It is easy to get hung up on organizing and preparing study materials, so set a time limit on this section of one or two hours. Otherwise, it is easy to put off studying by organizing, rereading, outlining, and re-outlining material instead of actively studying it.

- It is also important to view the planning and organizing stage as a valid study session, so it should not be done in front of the television or while visiting with friends. When taken seriously, the planning stage can help familiarize you with the information.

- Take the organization time to determine which main points need to be studied and then find notes from lectures and other materials that go with each main point.

- The planning session is a time to develop study sheets such as concept maps, note cards, questions, outlines, and tests as well as to answer the study guide questions and predict essay exam questions that will be used later in the study schedule. Active studying strategies and necessary materials will be discussed in the next chapter.

- The planning session also requires you to block out time each day to study the materials and list what will be studied each day. Some students like to study one section of the material each day with a final review at the end, while others prefer to study all the material using a different method each day with a final review at the end.

- Realize the importance of not planning a study session immediately preceding the exam. It helps the brain to get ready for the exam to do something relaxing such as listening to music, visiting with friends, going for a walk, or doing anything else that is fun to give the brain time to think about the information without cramming.

See the Future and Predict Questions

This is another part of your detective work. If you're lucky, the professor might even hand out the questions that will be on the exam. They do want you to succeed, after all. Sometimes, the list will literally be a *copy of the exam.* Other times, it is a database of questions from which the professor will pull questions for the exam. In these cases, study your heart out with the wonderful guidelines your professor has bestowed upon you.

In most cases, though, professors are not this generous, and it is important for students to predict which questions will be on the exam to help them know what to study.

You should estimate that there will be about four or five times the number of questions that will be on the actual exam. This way, you can be fully prepared to answer almost *any question.* Before getting to work, it is important to know what types of questions to ask.

Tip #79

For objective tests, questions should be specific and include definitions, dates, people, key concepts, and formulas. Anything that is bolded, highlighted, or in the margins of the textbook as well as main points in the lecture notes is a great place to start. Another place to find information is in the key terms at the end of the chapters and any key terms suggested during lectures.

Subjective, or essay exams focus more on general topics. These questions can be made from the main points in the lecture and textbook, but also focus on application from the questions and may require the students to tie together two or more main points. Predicted subjective questions should emulate this.

All in all, you can never truly "predict" the questions that will be on the exam. Most of the time though, your professor will (at the very least) *hint* towards what topics will be on the exam. Your job then is to nail every aspect of this topic so you can become a confident expert on it.

Utilize Provided Resources

Many students arrive at college with the idea that they are on their own. What they do not realize is colleges and universities, while learning institutions at heart, are also "businesses" in the sense that they need to succeed to stay afloat. The best way to prove success for colleges and universities is to promote the success of their students. Although they're not throwing out A's like confetti in a parade for students to gleefully collect, they create a plethora of resources to help them earn successful grades.

So, are colleges more difficult and want you to actually learn things? Yes. Do they want you to succeed? Yes, yes, and yes.

The first step is to find out what study-help resources are available to you. This can be found by visiting the dean of students' office, the library, the advising center, or the student information office in the student union. These resources include the following:

- *Writing Centers.* English majors and English graduate students act as writing tutors and staff the writing centers. You can go to the writing center for help throughout the writing process or with a draft for review.

- *Testing Review Rooms.* Some universities have a room, often in the library, which contains files of old tests from professors. You can find the tests and use them as study guides.

- *Tutor Labs.* Most universities offer tutoring labs where you can sign up for tutoring sessions in whichever subject you need. You are paired with majors and graduate students to help you through the information, and labs are often flexible in terms of the number of meetings per week and times of the sessions.

Tip #80

Ask your professor for help.

Trust us, you'll want to use it! The professor is taking his or her time to help you, so if no one seeks it out, then that's precious time wasted. Your professors will sometimes offer the following three things:

- *Study Sessions.* Professors often schedule a study session in the evening the night before or a few nights before an exam. You're allowed to come with questions and often the professor will go over key concepts that will appear on the exam.

- *Study Groups.* Some professors organize study groups or set up a time and place for interested students to meet to study for an exam.

- *Study Guides.* Professors sometimes hand out study guides that list the information needed to do well on the exam. You should study all the information on the guide since it will likely appear on the exam.

Active Studying Strategies

Simply reading and rereading notes is not enough for most students to do well. To learn and understand the information, successful students find active studying strategies to be the most prudent. While most students find a few of these strategies that they like the best, it is also important to remember that many successful students use two or three different strategies when studying for each test be able to recall information more easily when under the pressure of the actual exam.

Summarize and Condense

Summarizing and condensing works for subjective exams that require you to have a general understanding of the information and be able to recall it and apply it, and generally does not require you to remember specific dates, numbers, or definitions. Throughout this process, put the information into your own words and restate it several times to really understand the concepts and main points. Continue summarizing and condensing the information until you are able to use a basic, keyword study sheet to help you recall information. Here is how it is done:

- Determine how many sheets are needed. The idea is to get one main point or concept on each sheet of paper. One way to determine this is to look at the syllabus to see which main points are listed. Sometimes there will be one main concept covered each day or each week. Another way is to make a sheet on each individual lecture and its accompanying reading assignment.

- List each main point or concept on the top of each sheet of paper.

- Go through all of the lecture and text notes and rewrite the appropriate information on each sheet. This can be done as a paragraph or as an outline.

One consideration for making these sheets is if the test is strictly essay questions and the professor provides a list of possible essay questions. Each sheet should cover one essay question. The information you add to the sheet should be the answer to the question.

At this point, the preparation work for this type of active studying is complete. There are several ways to use the sheets, but the basic premise is that you read and review the sheets until you can remember enough of the information to condense it down to one step. If it is a three-step outline, you can rewrite the outline leaving out the third step but still recalling the information when looking at the outline. If it is a paragraph, you should condense the paragraph into fewer sentences. Continue to condense the information until all you have left is a basic form of the original that still has the keywords. As you review this basic sheet, you can recall the details related to each keyword.

Use Flash Cards

Now that you've mastered summarizing and condensing information for the subjective exam, we move onto a strategy for the objective exam: flash cards. Most tests will be a combination of subjective and objective content. That is, they'll ask you to apply concepts in your own way *and* recall specific details about events, objects, or people, keywords, definitions, etc. Creating flashcards is a great way to get these details down and you can even save them for finals week!

Flashcards are successful study aids for all subjects. Here are some examples:

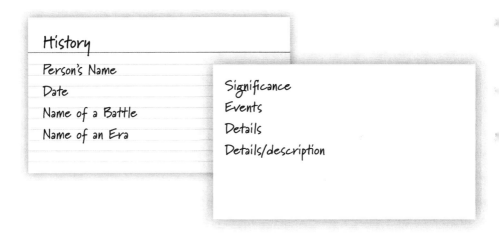

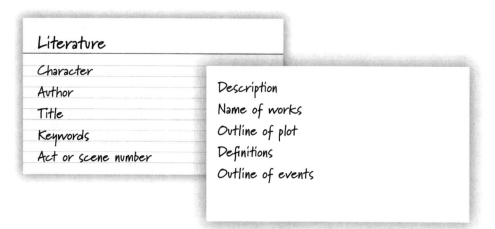

Literature

Character	Description
Author	Name of works
Title	Outline of plot
Keywords	Definitions
Act or scene number	Outline of events

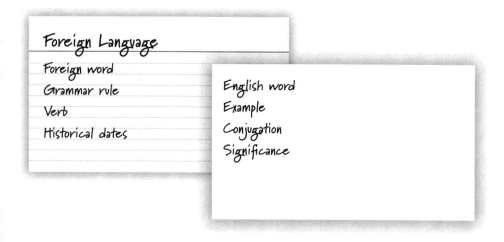

Foreign Language

Foreign word	English word
Grammar rule	Example
Verb	Conjugation
Historical dates	Significance

Tip #81

Here's a multi-part tip that will walk you through the process of making, using, and reviewing your flashcards in the most effective way:

- *Make them early.* Students who want to thoughtfully prepare make flashcards throughout the semester so they are ready when it is time to study for an exam. One way to quicken this process is to highlight or mark key information in the notes and then go back and convert the information to the flashcard.

- *Use the space.* Successful students use both the front and back of the flashcards. One side has a keyword or concept and the other side has the definition or explanation. This way they can study the information from both sides.

- *Master a few at a time.* Successful students do not overwhelm themselves with trying to master 100 flashcards in one sitting. They carry the cards with them and try to master 15 or 20 at a time. Then they move onto the next set while taking time to review the already mastered sets periodically.

- *Group them accordingly.* Successful students find a logical way to group the flash card whether it is by lecture topic or type of card (as indicated by the type of information on side one in the chart).

- *Review appropriately.* Successful students take the time to review the entire collection of flashcards one last time before the exam.

Use Visual Depictions of Information

Visual depictions can be great study aids for *both* subjective and objective tests. The options for these depictions include maps, timelines, charts, graphs, diagrams, and cluster maps. Similar to the two previous methods, the information on the visual depictions should be grouped by main point or concept if they are being used to cover all of the information to be studied.

The difference with visual depictions is they do not need to cover all of the information if you use them along with another active study method. For example, a timeline may be appropriate to help you remember the details of part of a larger event that you're studying. You can also use visual depictions to help tie the main points together, such as using a cluster map to figure out how seemingly unrelated historical events led up to one significant historical event.

Most of the time, you can't draw pictures and expect to remember all the important facts. Rather, to be successful you should use visual depictions in many different ways to aide in your studying. You can:

- Use the visual depictions to help you grasp a concept and write your own version of the concept down for studying as either a summary sheet or a flash card.

- Summarize and condense the visual depictions similar to how you summarize and condense outlines and paragraphs.

- Create diagrams on the flash cards with a description on the back.

- Continually review the visual depiction.

- Rest assured that the act of creating the visual depiction was a great study experience in and of itself.

Create a Study Group

Maybe you learned to hate study groups in high school for many good reasons. No one showed up. Or one person was a control freak. Or maybe, you're just a lone wolf and prefer to do work that you can fully call your own. For students who don't know how to use them correctly, study groups can be a hindrance instead of a help. Here are some helpful hints that you can use to make study groups your greatest asset:

- *Jumpstart study groups.* About a week before the exam, study groups can work together to predict questions and share their predictions with each other. This is a great way to streamline the process.

- *End with a review session.* Peers are great for reviewing as well. Use a final group review session to quiz one another and discuss the concepts the day before the exam. This is also a great time to have others help clear up misunderstandings.

- *Know whom to avoid.* Sometimes study groups have people who do not do any work on their own and expect to glean off of the hard workers in the group. Successful students know to excuse themselves from this group to either go study alone or find a different group.

- *Balance leadership and teamwork.* Study groups need to stay on task and they need a leader to keep them on task. The leader needs to remember, though, this is a group of peers so it is important to not become a dictator of how they spend their time.

Master the Review

Review sessions will reflect your hard work and be an essential step in studying for your exams. By this time, you have prepared your study materials and spent several study sessions actively studying the material. The last study session before the test should be *a review* instead of trying to cram in more new information.

Fun Fact

A UCLA study found that spacing out study sessions was more effective for students than cramming 90 percent of the time. Yet 73 percent of the students still believed that cramming was better.

These review sessions should not occur immediately before the class, but can occur the night before or earlier in the day. There are many different ways to review. Successful students may:

- Recreate their study sheets and compare the new one with the original.

- Make one last pass through the flashcards.

- Take a self-created test using the questions predicted earlier.

- Take an old test from the test collections at the university.

- Recite information on the study sheets.

- Write out answers to possible essay questions.

- Explain visual depictions to study partners or study groups.

Whatever method successful students use, they make sure they have gone over all the information one last time and do not use this time to try to learn new information. The review session should be proof to you that you know the information and are prepared for the upcoming exam. It's simply checking what you know, breathing in, breathing out, and accepting that you've done your best.

Chapter 9

What Kind Of Exam Is It?

There will be many kinds of exams professors will throw at you in college, some of which you may have never seen before. This chapter lays out what you'll expect to see crop up on these different types of exams and how to strategize accordingly.

Take the Objective Exam

Objective exams can induce a humongous sigh of relief in the worried student. Basically, all of the correct information is already there on the page, you just have to find it! Objective questions do not require the student to have total recall of the information, just the ability to recognize accurate information. The downfall is when there are answers that look just a little too similar to one another and you start getting tripped up and doubtful when faced with the choices.

Make the Right Choice

Tip #82

When completing multiple-choice exams, develop a plan that works for you. Look over all the questions and answer the ones you know first. Then, work on the remaining questions.

Here are some hints that successful students use to help them get past the difficult questions they encounter:

Example: The first step in successfully taking an exam is to:

A. The keywords.

B. Answer the easy questions first.

C. Budget the time.

D. Read the directions.

E. All of the above.

- *Look for grammatical errors.* If the possible answer does not grammatically match up with the stem, then it can be discarded as a correct answer. For example, "A" does not grammatically fit with the stem so it can be thrown out as an option.

- *Read all possibilities.* There may be a good answer to the question and a better answer to the question. In the above example, you may read "B" and think it is a good answer, and it is a good answer. However, "D" is the best answer because you need to read the directions before you know how to answer even the easy questions correctly.

- *Underline keywords and phrases.* This helps you focus on the details that may eliminate some possible answers. In the above question, you should underline "first step" to help you focus on the absolute first step, not just one of the first steps.

- *Make statements.* Another tip is to make the question and each possible answer into a statement and then determine if the statement is true or false. The ones you know for sure are false can be eliminated. In the above example, the statements would be:

A. The first step in successfully taking an exam is to the keywords.

B. The first step in successfully taking an exam is to answer the easy questions first.

C. The first step in successfully taking an exam is to budget the time.

D. The first step in successfully taking an exam is to read the directions.

Choice "A" is not grammatically correct so it has been eliminated and "B" and "C" are both false and "D" is true so it is the correct choice.

- *Answer before looking.* Some successful students try to answer the question before looking at the alternatives so they do not confuse themselves with the distractors.

- *Deal with "all of the above."* This possible answer can be eliminated if there is one answer that you know for sure is wrong. Likewise, if two possible answers are right, it is likely the correct answer is "all of the above" even if you are unsure about the remaining options. You can apply the same logic to "none of the above" options.

- *When all else fails, guess.* Successful students know leaving a question blank is a way to get zero points, but putting an answer (any answer) in the blank, even if it is a guess, is better than nothing.

Find the Truth

True or false questions can stump the most successful students because they often find themselves second-guessing their first instinct. There are hints and tips to help get through these sections on tests, however.

- The most important thing to remember for true or false tests is the entire statement must be true for the answer to be true. If there is one word that makes the statement false or even partially false, then the answer has to be false.

- Underline keywords and phrases in true or false statements to help you look for parts of the statement that may be false. Some examples of important keywords include names, dates, numbers, places, and titles.

- Be aware that absolute words such as "always," "none," "only," and "never" may render the statement false because there are often exceptions to the rule.

- You should also be aware of the qualifying words such as "some," "usually," "often," "may," "many," and "can" that often render an otherwise false statement true because it leaves room for exceptions.

- Look for a word or an omission of a word that makes the statement false.

- Correct the false statements if you have time, to remind you of why you marked it false in the first place. This is a great way to show the professor why you marked the statement as you did in case there is a question of validity of the answer.

- Know in the instances where you have to guess, you should put "true," because professors will often make more true statements than false statements.

Play Matchmaker

Matching tests seem straightforward and easy, but they can take a turn for the worse with one wrong answer. This is because most students make their choices and cross off the used options. If one of these options is wrong, it can throw off all of the following answers or require a lot of reworking to fix mistakes. There is nothing worse for students working to finish an exam on time than having to erase all the answers and markings and start from scratch in a matching section. Use the following tips to help you quickly and efficiently get through the matching sections on exams:

- Working from the side with the most words can be faster than the other way around because you have fewer words to scan through when choosing the correct "match."

- The best way to start is to make one pass-through of all the options and only mark the answers you know with certainty. This will eliminate a number of options for the less certain options.

- Continue to go through and mark answers that can be made with certainty based on which options are left. The second pass-through will yield a few more answers based on the eliminated options from the first time, and so on for each pass-through of all the remaining options.

- If you get to a point where you cannot make any more certain answers, then it is time to eliminate the possibilities that are not correct. After that, you should guess.

- Finally, it is important to do a quick read-through to make sure there were no clerical errors in marking the answers.

Take the Essay Exam

Essay exams can be a little more daunting than objective exams because they often ask you to apply the information in new ways. This means you must have a deeper understanding of the information and how the different concepts and main points relate to one another.

The first step in completing an essay exam is to carefully read the directions. This will tell you how many questions to answer, how long the answers should be, what extra information must be turned in such as outlines and notes, and what format you should use such as writing only on one side of the paper or skipping lines. You can read the chapter in the next section called "Understanding Directive Words" to help you decode essay exam questions.

To be a successful student, you should also:

- Refrain from answering more than the assigned number of questions. This allows you to focus your energy on the number that will be graded.

- Look for clues when there is not a specified length. Essay or short answer questions that only leave one-third or one-quarter of the page are not asking for more than a few sentences for an answer. Questions that have one or more pages are looking for longer, more in-depth answers.

- Read through all of the questions before starting to answer them so you can choose the questions you are most qualified to answer.

- Plan with a short outline and a few notes before writing.

- Avoid a rough draft since there is rarely time to write a final draft. Thus, take the necessary steps to ensure proper organization and neatness the first time through.

- Do not discard your experience with the writing process. You may condense the steps, but they are all still there. This means you create a thesis statement, write an outline, and draft the essay. Then, if there is still time, you can do a quick editing session to catch any major errors.

- Answer the questions instead of simply writing down all of the information you know about the topic.

- Keep the essay neat and easy to read by using margins, neat penmanship, and blue or black ink unless something else is specified in the directions. This is important because it makes the professor happy during the grading process.

Above all, make sure you turn in a well-written piece that is focused and organized.

Take the Open Book Exam

Open book exams, a variation on the traditional essay exams, sound like a breeze. Most students hear "open book" and lay back in their seats with a tropical drink. This is a grave mistake for students who are inexperienced in the practice of open book exams. Open book exams are often more difficult than traditional exams and are meant to test your ability to use, apply, and think about the information instead of your ability to memorize and repeat facts. Open book exams require critical thinking and the ability to construct and support arguments with facts.

Preparation is key when it comes to open book exams. You need to know where to find the facts you need to back up your arguments, opinions, and use of the key concepts discussed. A great way to study for an open book exam is to create study sheets similar to the summarizing and condensing activity. It is not as necessary to memorize the information as it is to be familiar with it and know how to apply it.

Before going to an open book exam, successful students get clear notes from the professor about what they are and are not allowed to bring to the test. Some professors put no limits, while others only allow one notebook or textbook. Sometimes you may only bring in a specific number of sheets of paper filled with notes.

Open book exams can be overwhelming if you have not experienced them, but here are some great tips for successful students:

- *Less is more.* It is possible to bring too much information into the test. The test is often timed so there is not enough time to go through piles and piles of resources. This is where preparation helps. Often, one or two textbooks and good notes are the keys to successful supplies.

- *Make a cheat sheet.* If you're allowed to bring in your own notes, you'll find it useful to have a cheat sheet of main points, important dates, key formulas, or other relevant information for quick access during the exam.

- *Read carefully.* This includes both directions and exam questions. The directions will give information on the required format of the exam, while the questions will explain what type of information is requested. You should refer to the "Understand Directive Words" chapter for more information on how to answer specific types of questions.

- *Quote the experts.* When answering the essay questions, quote the book and other experts covered in class materials to back up your answers. You also know the professor is not looking for an answer copied right out of the book so, include your own ideas, opinions, and analysis.

- *Put your main focus on content.* Some students struggle with answering essay questions because they are perfectionists when it comes to writing. This is a difficult habit to break, but with the time constraints often present in open book exams, you should put priority on content and worry about style later. This does not mean you need to disregard all of your writing skills, it means you do not have to write a stellar metaphor when a plain comparison does the trick. Another example is using a regular word instead of taking the time to look up the "perfect" word in a thesaurus, or spending unnecessary time racking your brain for one.

- *Know when to stop.* Most open book exams are designed with limits — either page limits, time limits, or both. This means you need to be able to state your answers concisely and accurately. Successful students aim for concise, accurate, and thoughtful answers based on evidence.

There is another less common type of open book exam; these exams are take-home exams where the professor assigns questions and gives students a certain amount of time outside of class to complete the answer. These tests do not require as much preparation before the exam, but they do require a thorough use of materials to answer the posed question. Although it's tempting to not study for these, you'll still need to review class material so you can access it with ease, because chances are you'll have at least a couple of other exams you'll need to study for!

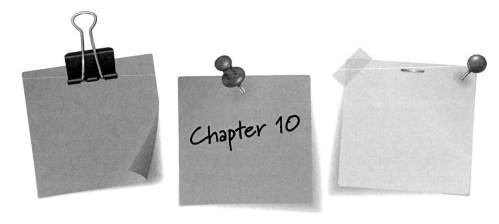

Chapter 10

Review Returned Tests

S o, the exam is over. Most students, other than looking at their grade, ignore the scored exam entirely. This piece of paper caused them so much stress and worry, so why would they want to spend more time on it than they already have? What they do not realize is they are foregoing an easy task that can be one of the most successful practices to help them improve their grade or ensure continued success on future exams in the class.

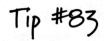

Tip #83

Take an hour or two to review all of your returned tests, and analyze how well your study methods worked and where they failed.

Look at Mistakes

Successful students take the time to go over their mistakes. You should do this for a few reasons: First, it helps you note what types of information you either did not study or studied wrong. It also helps you see if you need help mastering a certain concept before moving on to something new in the course. Looking at the mistakes also helps you see if you made careless errors or if you misread the directions. Since professors tend to find an exam style and stick with it, this review of errors will help when taking future exams. Finally, going over the mistakes helps you see what type of information the professor looks for, especially on short answers and essay questions.

- Successful students go one step further and take the time to find out and understand the correct answer. If you cannot figure out the right answer or understand why your answer was wrong, you should go to the professor seeking an explanation and help in understanding the correct answer.

- Successful students also look for the right answer in notes from the text and the lectures to check their note-taking accuracy. If you strictly studied your notes and the information was wrong in the notes, then you know to do more careful note-taking in the future.

- Successful students make notes of the areas of information they missed on the exam so they know what needs to be relearned instead of just reviewed for comprehensive exams later in the semester.

Read and Understand Comments

Successful students make sure they can read and understand the comments written on the exam. If you cannot read or do not understand, you know to plan a visit to the professor for clarification. This is important because these comments often give great insight on what types of information the professor looks for and helps you know what to include in the future:

- Comments that say, "You *might* have . . ." mean, "You *should* have . . ." or, "In the future you may try . . ." means, "In the future you *should* try . . ."

- Professors also comment on the use of details by telling when and where you need more details, and when and where you need to be more general in their answers.

- They also may point out patterns in errors such as, "It looks like you might be confusing X and Y by the way you are answering these questions."

- Professors may not fully understand your answers and may make a request to see you to discuss it. They will not try to track you down to have this discussion, but will leave it up to you to find the them and initiate the discussion.

Professors also make comments about the format of the exam and on your test-taking procedures that will help you evaluate and alter your testing strategies for the next test:

- A comment on a test that says the professor could not read your handwriting is a clue that you need to slow down and be neat.

- Comments may point out an error in how you followed directions, and since professors tend to use the same basic format for all tests, this helps you know what to look for in the future.

- Professors may also give you hints on which parts of the test to focus on first if the test was not completed in the time allotted.

All in all, professors vary widely in the kind of feedback they'll give you. Usually, if you did a good job, they'll have less to give. If you did poorly and they didn't say much, you may need to identify the problems yourself and then approach them for clarification. Again, they want you to do well, so no matter what concern you have with your test, you should feel free to approach them and ask.

Part IV: Completing Assignments

So far, we've gotten you through exams. Now, we'll move onto a whole other beast—completing assignments. Instead of the countless worksheets and chapter reviews you've completed in high school, you'll see more papers, presentations, and big projects. These are larger loads of a lesser frequency. It's important to understand effective approaches, because they will account for a high percentage of your grade. It's a little difficult to get used to, but once you follow a couple of pointers laid out in the next part of the book, you'll be on your way to wowing your professors with your flawless assignments.

Understand Directive Words and Phrases

Most students are used to being "cram bots." Just gather all these facts and put them in the right place and presto! There's an automatic "A," just because there are so many facts.

In college, this doesn't work a lot of the time. Understand that facts in college mean nothing without your own analysis and interpretation. For whatever reason, this isn't valued as much in high school, but it's a huge deal. Your professors are also researchers, who know *tons of facts*. What they don't know is what you think of them and how you can push them in new directions.

So, for assignments, professors will ask you to use the information they have researched in a specific way. This request is often in the assignment description in the form of **directive words and phrases**.

Tip #84

Decode these directive words and phrases so you can understand what type of project you are to complete, what type of information you are to include, and what type of approach you should take with completing the project.

Decoding Level One Directive Words

There are three levels of directive words in all. Level One directive words often require you to give information about a specific topic. This type of project requires research for facts and rarely asks for analysis, interpretation, or opinions of the topic. For instance, a statement like "George Bush was a terrible president" isn't 100 percent provable, so you wouldn't include this information in response to a level one directive word. Put your Clark

Kent glasses on and approach these types of projects like a reporter sniffing out "just the facts."

Describe. These assignments request that you write a detailed description of the topic. These assignments should follow a logical sequence and use plenty of examples to "show" the professor or audience what you are describing.

Example: Choose and describe five learning styles.

- Keywords: The keywords are "five" and "describe".

- Description: Successful students choose their topics and write about them in a way that "shows" the professor or other audience what each learning style is using examples. You may describe the characteristics of people with these learning styles, in what situations the learning style is useful, and in what situations the learning style has proven to be problematic.

- Warnings: The assignment prompt is not asking you to judge or evaluate the learning styles, so you should provide an impartial description of each one. It's okay to include interesting *facts,* but not opinions.

- Format: Unless otherwise noted, "describe" assignments generally look for answers in paragraph form. Paragraphs will be organized according to "categories" of information. First, you might introduce what a learning style *is* and a list of what learning styles there are. Then, go through systematically describing each one.

Research. Assignments requesting you to research a topic are telling you to go beyond the information presented in class and found in assigned readings. The professor wants you to dig deeper to get a more thorough understanding of the topic.

Example: Research the implications of not determining and developing a preferred learning style.

- Keywords: The keywords are "research," "implications," and "not."

- Description: You are *not* looking for information about a learning style of your choice. Instead, you are looking for examples that describe what happens to students who do not know their preferred learning style and what can happen as a result.

- Warnings: Some students may not carefully read the prompt and miss the "not" in the directions. Other students may spend a good portion of the assignment describing the learning style, but the prompt says to write about the implications, so you should assume the audience knows what the learning styles are.

- Format: The format is not noted in this instance. Answers to research prompts can be listed, written in paragraph form, or diagramed. If you are unsure, you should consult with the professor for further details.

Define. Assignments requesting you to define the topic are asking you to give the topic's meaning according to someone or a specific source. Sometimes the source is specified. When it is not specified, successful students know to look for information in a few sources to find the most accurate description or definition possible.

Example: Define three learning styles based on the information given in the text.

- Keywords: The keywords are "define," "three," "learning styles," and "text."

- Description: Successful students know they need to go to the text to find the information needed to complete this assignment. Look over information and devise your own definition based on what the book says.

- Warnings: Some students may copy the information from a source, but in most cases, the professor is looking for them to define the requested terms in their own words. To define a term in your own words you need to be able to fully understand it first.

- Format: In most instances, the prompt to define a term means the answer will be only a few sentences. There are cases, however, where the professor asks the term be defined in a longer format. In such cases, you should look for various ways to define a term including breaking the topic into smaller sections and defining each individual section.

Explain a process. Assignments requesting you to explain a process are similar to the "describe" and "define" prompts. Successful students know explaining a process requires them to look at all aspects of the topic and give full details for each one and organize it in a sequential manner.

Example: Explain the process of determining a learning style.

- Keywords: The keywords are "explain," "process," and "learning style."

- Description: First, find information about the steps to determine a learning style and then give details and examples for each step.

- Warnings: Some students may think listing the steps is enough, but listing the steps and explaining the background, examples, and possible road blocks for each step gives more explanation than a simple, one sentence step.

- Format: The assignments for "explain a process" prompts can be written in a step-by-step list as long as the steps include explanations. Some professors may require that the information be written out in paragraph form; however, this means each step would be a paragraph in the finished project.

Enumerate/List. Assignments requesting you to enumerate or list want you to recall keywords, examples, or steps in a process. These types of assignments are not looking for long explanations of the items in the list, only the basic information.

Example: List the steps a student should use to determine their learning style.

- Keywords: The keywords are "list," "steps," and "learning style."

- Description: You should know you need to recall, locate, or determine the steps students should take when they want to know what learning styles they prefer. You also know you do not need to describe the steps, and instead list them accordingly.

- Warnings: Some students do not take a listing prompt seriously because it sounds easy and straightforward. For the most part, it is fairly straightforward, but you need to take the time to ensure you list all of the necessary points and do not miss anything important.

- Format: This assignment should be presented in a numerical list. If it is a process, the items should be listed chronologically.

Summarize. Assignments requesting you to summarize want you to take a large amount of information and condense it down into your own words. This shows the professor you understand the material enough to write it in your own words and that you are able to pick out the most important points.

Example: Summarize the characteristics of three different learning styles.

- Keywords: The keywords are "summarize," "three," and "learning styles."

- Description: Successful students choose three of the given learning styles and summarize their characteristics. To do this, pick out the main points under each one and explain them in a brief paragraph.

- Warnings: Some students see the word summarize and make one of two mistakes. The first mistake that some students make is copying one or more sentences from their sources that seem to describe the topic. The other common mistake for summarizers is putting the information into their own words but missing important details. You should know it is important to put the information into your own words and to make sure you have covered all of the main points.

- Format: Unless the assignment directs otherwise, a summary is written in paragraph form. Also, if there is no length requirement given in the assignment, you can gauge the length by allowing about one paragraph for each page of information that is summarized.

Diagram. Assignments requesting you to diagram want you to gather information and create a visual depiction of some sort. This diagram can be a chart, graph, timeline, cluster map, or other visual representation of the information. Sometimes the type of visual representation is specified and other times it is left up to you to decide what will work the best.

Tip #85

Make sure you read directions — take a moment to really digest what each and every question is asking of you. Don't lose points because you misinterpreted a question.

Example: Diagram the learning styles discussed in class to highlight their shared characteristics.

- Keywords: The keywords are "diagram," "learning styles," and "shared characteristics."

- Description: Successful students know they will be able to choose which type of visual depiction they will use. They also know they need to come up with a list of characteristics for each learning style and then see which learning styles share which characteristics. There are several ways to do this. You can make a chart with the learning styles across the top and the characteristics down the side and place checkmarks in the corresponding squares to illustrate which learning styles have which characteristic. Another option is to make a cluster map that has every characteristic listed as a cluster center with the corresponding learning styles coming off of each cluster.

- Warnings: Some students use the same type of visual depiction time after time. This is not the most efficient way to display the information in all cases, however. For example, a timeline would not be effective in this instance.

- Format: The assignment format depends on the type of visual depiction chosen, but an important thing to remember regardless of the type of depiction is it should be neat and orderly. The use of colors can help highlight certain areas of the chart, but you should be careful to not make it too busy.

Trace. Assignments requesting you to trace a topic want you to show a progression through time, whether it is a process, an event, or a transformation.

Example: Trace the events leading up to the discovery of learning styles.

- Keywords: The keywords are "trace," "up to the discovery," and "learning styles."

- Description: Successful students know they need to look at what prompted researchers to look into the possibility of learning styles and what they did to pinpoint the different kinds of learning styles.

- Warnings: Students who do not read the prompt carefully may not trace the right set of events.

- Format: Unless specified, there are several different ways to present this information. Prompts, such as this one, could be presented as a timeline. Other possible formats are lists, steps, and paragraphs.

Outline. Assignments requesting you to outline are instructing you to pick out the main points or key events. These assignments work well to show basic understanding of a complex theory or concept. They also work well when you need to demonstrate understanding and comprehension of reading assignments.

Example: Outline the characteristics and pros and cons of one learning style.

- Keywords: The keywords are "outline," "characteristics and pros and cons," and "learning style."

- Description: Successful students know they have to create a three part outline for this assignment using the three main points listed in the prompt, each with its own main points and details. They also know they have to plan an organizational method that shows fairly equal levels of detail for each main point.

- Warnings: Students who struggle with outlining make one of two mistakes: The first mistake is not using an organizational method. Students fail to plan out how deeply they will go into the outline and are unable to keep their organization consistent. The second mistake is giving too much detail. This type of assignment should contain the main points and essential details, but minor details should be left out of the final project.

- Format: This project should be presented in an outline format.

Identify. Assignments requesting you to identify are asking you to name something specific. These prompts may clarify how many items need to be identified or in what manner they should be presented.

Example: Identify in a short paragraph five methods students can use to develop their verbal learning skills.

- Keywords: The keywords are "identify," "paragraph," "five," and "verbal learning skills."

- Description: Successful students know they will need to find or recall information on verbal learning skills and write a paragraph about how students can help develop their skills. You do not need to include your opinions or justifications, but simply list the items asked for.

- Warnings: Some students may take the time to evaluate the merit of each of these methods, but this is not what the question is asking. Another error is not clearly reading the prompt that tells you to write the answer in paragraph form.

- Format: While this prompt asks for a paragraph, some identify assignments do not specify or instead, ask for a list of items.

Comment. Assignments requesting you to comment are asking you to discuss a specific portion of the topic in a clear, concise, and organized manner. The assignments assign a specific sub-topic or give a choice of sub-topics to discuss.

Example: Comment on the common struggles of visual learners in college-level classes.

- Keywords: The keywords are "comment," "struggles," and "visual learners."

- Description: Successful students know they need to write about the problems visual learners have in class.

- Warnings: A careless mistake with this type of prompt occurs when students fail to limit their answers to the specifications in the prompt. In this example, a mistake is not limiting answers to struggles in class. Another common mistake is when students evaluate and judge the comments instead of making the statements.

- Format: This prompt looks for a written answer in paragraph form. The length of the answer depends on the amount of information to be commented on. In this instance, a paragraph would suffice.

Decipher Level Two Directive Words

Level Two directive words ask you to take the information one step further than presenting the facts in a specific manner. These types of assignments require you to interpret information and find ways to make connections about the topic or more sub-points of the topic. Projects at this level include an equal mixture of facts and personal connections and interpretations. It is important for you to remember, however, that all connections and interpretations should be backed by credible sources.

Discuss. Assignments requesting you to discuss want you to examine the topic and talk about the validity, pros and cons, or benefits and disadvantages of it. Discussing a topic is showing all sides of it in an impartial manner, but it takes analyzing skills to be able to come up with and organize the information properly.

Example: There were three main benefits to determining learning styles presented during class lectures. Discuss these benefits.

- Keywords: The keywords are "three," "benefits," and "discuss."

- Description: Successful students know they need to recall the information presented in the lecture and think about the validity of each of the benefits. State your opinions about the validity of the benefits and back them up with explanations from the lecture, other sources, and reasoning.

- Warnings: Discussing prompts want you to show all sides of the issues so you need to take care to not write a one-sided or weighted answer to the questions.

- Format: The discussion is most often presented in paragraph form. In this instance, there are three paragraphs, one for each of the benefits listed.

Compare. Assignments requesting you to compare will ask you to take two or more seemingly different topics and find and discuss similarities. In some cases, the similarities are obvious and in other cases, the similarities are not obvious until you have examined and analyzed the topics.

Example: Compare the intuitive learner with the verbal learner.

- Keywords: The keywords are "compare," "intuitive learner," and "verbal learner."

- Description: Successful students know they need to find thorough descriptions of these two types of learners and think about the characteristics for each one. You need to draw conclusions about these characteristics to see where the similarities lie.

- Warnings: Some students are easily frustrated when the similarities are not readily apparent. They fail to think critically about the topics and give up without giving the assignment a chance.

- Format: The most common way to present this information is in paragraph form, but you may prefer to use a Venn diagram to highlight the similarities.

Contrast. Assignments requesting you to contrast ask you to take two seemingly similar topics and highlight the differences. Similar to the compare prompts, sometimes the differences are fairly obvious and other times they are not apparent without a thorough examination of the topics.

Example: Contrast sensing learners with sequential learners.

- Keywords: The keywords are "contrast," "sensing learners," and "sequential learners."

- Description: Successful students know they need to look at the learning styles that have many similarities and think about what makes each one unique. Your finished assignment will show the learning styles are similar but have unique features.

- Warnings: Similar to the compare prompts, some students get frustrated when the requested information is not readily recognizable.

- Format: Contrast prompts result in the answers being written in paragraph form, but they can also be presented in a Venn diagram or a cluster map.

Illustrate. Assignments requesting you to illustrate are asking you to take a topic and come up with examples that show the audience the meaning of the topic. These examples can sometimes be found in lecture notes, texts, and other resources, but students who attempt to apply the topic or concept to their lives will be able to come up with unique illustrations of the topic.

Example: Illustrate the ways active learners and reflective learners can help one another.

- Keywords: The keywords are "illustrate," "active," "reflective," and "help."

- Description: Successful students know they need to look at the deficiencies of each of these types of learners and see if the advantages of the other type can fill the void in some way. You need to connect these relationships with specific examples.

- Warnings: Some students stop at the point where they have made the relationships. While this is an important step, you need to go one step further to illustrate what you are saying.

- Format: There are several ways you can present this information. You can write the information in paragraph or essay form or you could list each way and write out the example underneath it.

Apply. Assignments requesting you to apply the topic want you to take a concept or idea and show how it can work in different settings and situations. This type of project requires thorough understanding of the topic or concept to be able to show how it will function or react in a different or real-life setting.

Tip #86

Try to apply what you're learning to the world around you. This will make what you're studying more memorable.

For example, if you're in a psychology class and are learning about social mannerisms, such as mirroring, try to see if you can examine examples of this among your friends.

Example: Apply the steps for determining a learning style preference to yourself.

- Keywords: The keywords are "apply," "steps," "learning style," and "self."

- Description: Successful students know they need to take themselves through the steps to determine their individual learning style preferences. Explain how you worked through the steps and make a conclusion as to your learning style preference.

- Warnings: Some students may not actually apply the steps to their lives and instead go to the conclusion. While the conclusion is important, the professor uses this prompt to see that you understood the steps in the process, not only the end result.

- Format: The final project is an essay that explains how the process applied to your situation and also highlights the results.

Cause. Assignments requesting you to discuss the causes of a topic are asking you to explain the event or events that led up to another event. You need to be able to look at information and figure out which events are relevant to the topic and which may be concurrent but are not directly related.

Example: Sara is a physical learner who is constantly struggling in her study skills lecture. What are some causes for her struggles?

- Keywords: The keywords are "physical learner," "lecture," "possible," and "causes."

- Description: Successful students know they have to predict possible causes based on the information they know about physical learners and the reported struggles they have in lectures. The answer to this question is not found in the lecture notes or in the textbook, but the information leading to the answers will.

- Warnings: Some students may list the possible struggles that physical learners have, but if they fail to use the information to answer the question about Sara, they may lose points.

- Format: This type of prompt can often be answered in paragraph or list form.

Effect. Assignments requesting you to work with the effects of an event can ask you either to discuss what happened in a real situation as a direct result of one event, or they may ask you to predict what could happen in a hypo-thetical situation using the information you already know about the topic.

Example: Mike, a visual learner, began studying with Jane, a verbal learner. What are some possible effects of this relationship for each of them?

- Keywords: The keywords are "visual learner," "verbal learner," "effects," and "relationship."

- Description: Successful students know the first thing they need to do is see how the characteristics of visual learners can balance the characteris-tics of verbal learners and vice versa. You need to form your answer by showing how the relationship will affect Mike and then how it will affect Jane.

- Warnings: Some students determine how verbal and visual learners can balance each other, but they fail to specify the effects for each person, thus not answering the prompt.

- Format: The information for this prompt can be presented in a list or a paragraph. In this instance, since there are two people, the effects could also be presented in a Venn diagram.

Relate. Assignments requesting you to relate to topics are asking you to show the connections between two or more people, events, or concepts. The assignment asks you to illustrate these relationships through examples and illustrations.

Example: Relate global learners to sequential learners.

- Keywords: The keywords are "relate," "global learners," and "sequential learners."

- Description: Successful students take time to find quality descriptions of both types of learners and look for their similarities and differences. Use the information to explain how working together would be great for them and how they would clash when working together.

- Warnings: Some students may write the descriptions of each type of learner and fail to make the connections on how they are related to one another.

- Format: These types of prompts require answer to be written in paragraph form.

Demonstrate. Assignments requesting you to demonstrate are asking you to show or prove something about the topic. You can make this proof by mixing opinions and judgments with facts, figures, and citations from experts.

Example: Demonstrate how a struggling student may use learning styles to help improve their grades.

- Keywords: The keywords are "demonstrate," "struggling," "learning styles," and "improve."

- Description: Successful students know they have to look at the process of using learning styles along with the benefits of using learning styles, and mesh the two to explain how struggling students can benefit. Take the information and write an essay incorporating the information with proof in the form of facts, figures, and expert opinion.

- Warnings: Some students discuss the benefits of using learning styles and fail to apply it to struggling students along with the process. A demonstration prompt requires you to show your knowledge and prove its validity.

- Format: This type of prompt requires answers to be written out in essay or paragraph form.

Decipher Level Three Directive Words

Level Three directive words require you to do the most critical thinking out of all three types. These types of assignments ask you to evaluate and apply information. This is what professors *really* care about. These assignments require you to make a statement using evidence to back it up.

Review. Assignments requesting you to review want you to give a survey of the topic that praises the good points and criticizes the bad points. When you are asked to review a topic, the best thing you can do is think about a movie review and follow that format: include a quick summary, discuss the good points and bad points, then give an overall judgment.

Example: Review the use of learning styles by college students.

- Keywords: The keywords are "review" and "learning styles."

- Description: Successful students know they need to give a brief overview about the theory of learning styles, list the benefits of utilizing this theory with examples, list the disadvantages of utilizing this theory with examples, and then give an overall judgment as to whether or not they think the use of the learning styles theory is a good use of time for college students.

- Warnings: The review of good points and bad points should be a personal opinion backed up with expert opinion, proven examples, and logical reasoning. It should not be copied from a source.

- Format: Reviews are written in paragraph form.

Prove. Assignments requesting you to prove something will make a statement and then ask you to agree or disagree with it and then prove your side of the issue.

Example: Read the following statement, decide if you agree or disagree with it and then prove your side of the issue:

"Students who lean toward a verbal learning style are more likely to succeed in college than those who lean toward other learning styles."

- Keywords: The keywords are "read," "decide," and "prove."

- Description: Successful students know they need to make a decision of agreement or disagreement with the statement. Before you do so, you need to review the characteristics, advantages, and disadvantages of each type of learning style. Once you make your decision, look for examples, expert opinion, facts, and figures to show your decision is the best decision.

- Warnings: A common error for students is not taking one side but instead showing the pros and cons of both sides. Another common error on this type of assignment is not giving enough solid proof of your opinion and instead restating it in a variety of ways. Finally, a third common error is trying to prove your side of the issue with emotions instead of fact.

- Format: These assignments are written in essay or paragraph form.

Interpret. Assignments requesting you to interpret information want you to look at the information and explain its significance. You are also expected to include your thoughts and opinions on the information and back them up with facts and logical reasoning.

Example: "A recent study found that 62 percent of students who take a learning styles mini-course during their first semester of college graduate while only 47 percent of students who do not take the mini-course during their first semester of college graduate." You are provided with the rest of the study report including the methodology.

Interpret this study.

- Keywords: The keywords are "interpret" and "study."

- Description: Successful students know they need to read through the entire study and break it down into a few sub-topics. Once you have done that, you need to analyze the results and validity of each sub-topic. Then draw a conclusion about the study and back it up with information, facts, and reasoning.

- Warnings: Some students look at the results of the study and fail to look at the methodology, process, and other provided information about the study to make their interpretation. Other students fail to include their opinions and instead restate the findings without interpretation.

- Format: These assignments require the answer to be written in paragraph or essay form.

Evaluate. Assignments requesting you to evaluate want you to comment on the value of the topic. You are expected to explain the problem, issue, or topic, and discuss the advantages and disadvantages with a final recommendation.

Example: Evaluate the process of balancing the active and reflective learner.

- Keywords: The keywords are "evaluate," "process," and "active and reflective learner."

- Description: Successful students know they first have to explain the differences of active and reflective learning. Then, you should point out the problems for each type of learner if you cannot find a useful balance. Show the advantages and disadvantages of trying to strike a balance. Finally, make a final recommendation on whether or not it is useful to try to strike a balance between these two learning styles.

- Warnings: Some students list the characteristics, advantages, and disadvantages but they fail to take the final step of including their opinions about the value of the process.

- Format: These assignments are completed in paragraph or essay form.

Justify. Assignments requesting you to justify give you an opportunity to develop and state an opinion about a topic. Then, you are required to justify or prove why your opinion is valid by showing examples, expert testimony, comparisons, and reasoning.

Example: Decide whether or not you think using the theory of learning styles is an effective method to improve grades and study habits. Justify your answer.

- Keywords: The keywords are "learning styles," "effective," and "justify."

- Description: Successful students first take time to develop their opinion on the matter. Then, you should look for three to four main points to support your opinion and make sure you have examples, expert testimony, comparisons, studies, and reasoning to back up your opinion. From there, write a project that clearly states your opinion and uses a lot of sources to justify why your opinion is the best opinion.

- Warnings: Some students fail to use enough information to justify their opinion. The best way to overcome this obstacle is to make sure you have a variety of types of information from several sources.

- Format: This type of assignment is presented in paragraph or essay form.

Respond. Assignments requesting you to respond to a topic want you to state and back up your opinions. The response may be to a concept discussed in class as a whole or the professor may present a statement relating to a concept discussed in class and ask you to respond to it.

Example: Respond to the following statement:

"The best way for students to guarantee success in college is to determine their learning style and use this knowledge to their advantage."

- Keywords: The keywords are "respond," "guarantee," and "learning styles."

- Description: Successful students first spend time thinking about the statement and evaluating its validity. Once you have formed an opinion about the statement, you have to find reasons to back up this opinion. These reasons can be a variety of information including expert opinion, facts, figures, logic, or comparisons.

- Warnings: Some students fail to form a definitive opinion about the statement and tend to jump back and forth on both sides of the issue. Other students fail to take enough time to thoroughly back up their opinions.

- Format: This type of assignment is presented in paragraph or essay form.

Support or Oppose. Assignments requesting you to support or oppose want you to show the validity or invalidity of a concept or statement. The support can come in the form of examples, expert opinion, comparisons, and logical reasoning.

Example: Support or oppose the following statement:

"Students are out of luck if they have a learning style that does not meld with a professor's teaching style."

- Keywords: The keywords are "learning style," "teaching style," and "support or oppose."

- Description: Successful students know they need to decide if they want to support or oppose the statement. You need to gather and use evidence that agrees with your opinion.

- Warnings: Some students do not completely agree or disagree with the given statements so they have a difficult time working on the project. It is important to remember you do not need to agree with what you are writing as long as you present a solid support or opposition to the statement.

- Format: This type of assignment is presented in paragraph or essay form.

Analyze. Assignments requesting you to analyze want you to break down the subject into sections and go over the advantages and disadvantages of each section. The project should contain an overall conclusion about the topic after each section is thoroughly reviewed.

Example: Analyze the different learning styles.

- Keywords: The keywords are "analyze" and "learning styles."

- Description: Successful students know each learning style has to be treated as a sub-topic. You have to determine the pros and cons for each learning style, describe them in the assignment, and make a final conclusion about the learning styles. This conclusion could be about learning styles as a whole, the individual learning styles, or both.

- Warnings: Some students list the pros and cons of the learning styles and fail to use the information to draw a conclusion. This can result in a major loss of points since the conclusion is the part of the assignment that shows the professor what you think about the learning styles.

- Format: This type of assignment is presented in paragraph or essay form.

Argue. Assignments requesting you to argue want you to take a side on the issue, concept, or provided statement and prove why one side is more correct or more advantageous than the other side of the issue.

Example: Argue for or against the use of the theory of learning styles by college students.

- Keywords: The keywords are "argue" and "learning styles."

- Description: Successful students first have to decide if they think it is advantageous for students to use the theory of learning styles or not. Then, you have to determine the reasons for your opinion and gather information such as expert opinion, facts, figures, comparisons, and examples to help illustrate why your opinion is the most advantageous.

- Warnings: One of the biggest problems with arguing is some students fail to choose a side and jump back and forth, listing the pros and cons of both sides of the issue, without forming any sort of connection or conclusion.

- Format: This type of assignment is presented in paragraph or essay form.

Criticize. Assignments requesting you to criticize want you to make a judgment on the merit or correctness of a topic, concept, or statement. You are expected to analyze the topic by discussing the advantages and disadvantages and using the discussions to come to an overall conclusion about the merit of the topic.

Example: Criticize the learning style theory.

- Keywords: The keywords are "criticize" and "learning style theory."

- Description: Successful students know they need to decide whether or not the learning style theory is a valuable asset to college students. Once you decide on the merit value of the theory, show how its advantages and disadvantages support your opinion. Again, you do this through the use of expert opinion, facts, figures, comparisons, and logical reasoning.

- Warnings: Some students do a great job of listing the advantages and disadvantages and implying a side on the issue, but they fail to connect all the information together in a critical conclusion that shows their overall view of and answer to the prompt.

- Format: This type of assignment is presented in paragraph or essay form.

Handle Hybrid Directives

The previous examples show you how to approach assignment prompts that ask you to use one directive. There will be times, however, when assignment prompts will include two or more directives. The best way for you to handle these prompts is to progress through the directives starting with the level one directives then completing level two directives, and finally finishing up with the level three directives.

Tip #87

When a question has multiple parts, take care to answer it in its entirety. Don't ignore a secondary command because you're too hung up on the first part of a question.

Here are some examples:

- List and evaluate different learning styles. You should first list the learning styles and then move on to evaluating each one according to the information on how to evaluate a topic.

- Explain and review the process of determining a learning style preference. You should first list the steps in the process and then go back and fill in the review of each step. This prompt would be well served to have a final overall review at the end as well.

- Identify three disadvantages for and explain the effects of aural learning preferences. You should first determine the disadvantages and then move on to determine the overall effects of each disadvantage.

It is important for you to remember to cover all of the directives when completing the assignment so you do not lose points for the careless mistake of not following directions.

Special Considerations for Each Type of Assignment

There are three major types of assignments found in college courses. The last chapter was about understanding instructions, executing assignments, and, finally, how to organize according to what kind of operative commands were in the instructions. This chapter is about the larger categories of assignments and what most of the required tasks will be.

Research the Research Paper

Simply defined, a research paper is a paper that uses information from other sources to solve a problem. The degree of difficulty of a research paper varies depending on which level of directives the paper uses. Some research papers result from prompts containing level one directives because these directives require papers that are extremely research heavy. They contain few, if any, personal thoughts and opinions.

Paper prompts from level two directives are often research papers as well. While level two directives require more personal thought and analysis than level one, they often do not require the statement of opinions. Research papers rarely result from level three directives because these directives require the students to form and support opinions. Research papers in their purest form should be impartial accounts of the information.

There are many characteristics that help define effective research papers:

- *They contain researched, sourced, and cited material.* Failing to cite sources is considered plagiarism. It can result not only in academic repercussions from your institution but could also become a lawsuit. There are plenty of resources to help you create a bibliography with ease, such as the EasyBib add-on feature on Google Docs that allows you to cite as you go.

- *They are clear, concise, and well written.* This means they contain proper language, correct grammar and mechanics, and flow well. They are also easy to read and understand without being too simplistic. Basically, good research papers are the best approximations of truth. They don't leave anything out, but they don't go beyond what's completely true and necessary for the paper.

- *They contain an introduction, a body, a conclusion, and a works cited page or bibliography.* The professor may ask you to write on a variation of this form, but this is what research papers will always essentially be.

Here is an example of what a research prompt might look like:

"Research and summarize the findings of psychological studies on memory and concentration."

In this paper, you would need to create one or two sentences that summarize everything you've found (again, this is a fact, not an opinion) and present the research in a clear and organized way for the remainder of the copy.

Analyzing the Analysis Paper

Analysis papers are similar to research papers, but they contain more of the student's personal thoughts and opinions than research papers. Analysis papers result from level two and level three directives and are one-sided accounts. They state the topic, explain a position on that topic, present points with support that prove the position to be correct or advantageous, and conclude with a final recommendation and reiteration of the writer's original opinion of the topic.

Analysis papers will often require research to back up your claims, though not as much as a research paper, and is often more one-sided, driven by what you need to know to back up your argument. There will be instances when your will not need to research for an analysis paper, however. Sometimes, you may only use one source and argue for an interpretation. In literature, you may be asked to interpret a poem and use only sources from that poem to argue what you think it means.

Tip #88

Don't be afraid to think outside the box with your analysis. If you believe you can make a solid argument about how LeBron James uses physics, by all means, make your case. Analysis papers give you some more freedom.

It is also very rare that a professor will give you a broad category to write on. Rarely will you ever see: "Apples. Write about them!" Instead, they'll pick topics that are closely related to what you've learned in class and target specific areas. Here is a much more common question for a paper:

"In MLK's *Letter from Birmingham Jail*, what does light represent? Is it a religious symbol or a symbol of justice? Use examples from the text and additional research to back up your claim."

In this case, they want you to analyze the symbol of light using your own interpretation of the text and outside research.

Presenting the Presentation

Presentations are less common in college, especially in large lectures, but they're useful to know how to do. A presentation is usually based off of, even if indirectly, a research paper or an analysis paper. Even when you are not directed to write the paper as a specific part of the assignment, the "paper" is the written form of the presentation. Any level of directive can prompt presentations. Regardless of this directive, however, there are important steps successful students take to help promote success with the presentation:

- Successful students write out a script for every presentation even if they only use note cards during the actual presentation.

- Successful students prepare by reading and practicing their scripts and then moving to an outline. Eventually, through many rounds of practice, you will be able to recite your presentation using note cards containing a simple outline or keywords.

- Successful students know presentations need an introduction, body, and conclusion similar to papers.

- Successful students create handouts and visual aids that enhance their material. These can be visual depictions of the material such as timelines, charts, graphs, or maps.

Starting research

Research will almost always be necessary. Whether you use what's provided in class, or you have to use an academic database to find new sources, you'll find yourself always referring to solid evidence to come up with ideas. Even if it's a level-three or level-two directive, research will make you grounded and knowledgeable in the topic and inspire even more novel and exciting ideas that you can share in your assignments or in class.

Basically, you will always do a little bit of research for each and every assignment. And researching is usually the longest step in the process, which is why it's important to start early, get inspired, and know what you need to get from your sources to complete the assignment.

Start early

Tip #89

Don't let it sit on the burner until it catches on fire. Take advantage of time, and start early on your assignments. This doesn't always mean you're working on assignments weeks or months in advance, but start on it sooner than later in case things take longer than anticipated.

If you have a clear understanding of what is expected of you for the assignment, you can spend time thinking and brainstorming before you have to sit down and work on the assignment.

The first thing you should do is read through the assignment description. During this read-through, take preliminary notes and jot down any questions you may have about the assignment, the topic, or the format so that as soon as you have an opportunity to discuss the assignment with your professor, you have your questions ready.

At this point, to be successful you should:

- Pay attention to the details, such as the length, format, and any additional materials that will need to be developed.

- Determine which citation format you will be expected to use and find the necessary information if you are not familiar with the format.

- Figure out what types of sources you are required to use and determine whether or not your resources will be readily available.

- Discuss the assignment with students who have already taken the course with the same professor to get ideas about what the professor expects on assignments.

- Set arbitrary deadlines so you can work ahead and avoid the stress of the "night before it's due" cramming session.

- Make a plan to allow at least three days for the physical writing process for the paper or practicing for a presentation.

- Write your deadlines and plan into your schedule.

- Appreciate the value of thinking. Students who start early can spend a few days or weeks thinking about the topic can then get a better idea of what sources they'll use for their paper.

Choose a prompt

Most of the time, professors give you a choice for a prompt. This is a great opportunity for you because you have the chance to personalize the assignment as much as possible and, if you start early enough, you can think about your choices to pick one that interests you. Just like when you're making an important purchase, you may sometimes have a difficult time choosing a prompt.

You should first mark which prompt or prompts pop out to you as interesting. If nothing pops out as interesting, you should look at it from the other perspective and cross off the prompts you are not interested in using. Either way, you have narrowed the choices.

Writing is Only a Small Portion of the Success

One of the biggest mistakes that you can make when completing writing assignments is to fail to recognize that the actual writing part of the assignment is just a small percentage of the work necessary for a good grade. Successful students go through many steps and consider many options while completing their assignments. It may sound tedious or overwhelming at first, but successful students soon realize these steps and considerations become second nature to them and eventually writing assignments become easier.

Think about topics in relation to assignments

Successful students have realized that writing assignments rarely require them to simply write down all of the information they know about a topic. When you are given a specific question to answer or writing prompt to follow, you need to carefully read the assignment, consider the directive words, and make a plan to apply the information you have found about the topic in a way that answers the question or prompt presented to you.

Example: Compare the steps in the writing process presented by the author to the writing process that you currently use.

A mistake would be to simply describe everything about the writing process. A successful student knows that they need to look at the similarities and differences between their writing process and the author's writing process.

Some writing assignments are less specific and give a general topic or a type of paper and allow you the freedom to narrow your topics from there. Especially in these cases, you should carefully examine your topic and make sure it fits in the realm of the given assignment.

A thesis is a basis

The thesis is the most important sentence in any assignment. Contrary to what most people believe, thesis statements are not just for papers. They can be an extremely useful starting point for any assignment because they help you focus your ideas and decide how to proceed. Furthermore, theses act as a roadmap to help you stay focused as you proceed through the assignment.

When writing your theses statements, remember the statements need to be:

- *Concise.* Successful students know the thesis should clearly define information that they can present in the length of the assignment. For example, a thesis that requires the reader to describe WWII is not concise enough for a five-page paper. Instead, you would have to narrow the thesis to a specific battle, describing a specific cause, the reasons why a specific country joined the war, or the effects of the war on women in a certain part of the country.

- *General.* Successful students know the thesis should allow for enough information to be able to fill the minimum length requirements without redundancy. For example, a thesis about describing three places to research in the library probably will not provide enough information to fill a five-page paper, but it may be enough for a one-page paper.

- *Interesting and arguable.* This is especially true in instances when you have complete freedom over your topic. For example, a thesis about stating the differences between apples and oranges is not going to be interesting because most people already know the differences between apples and oranges. It also is not arguable because most people agree that apples and oranges are different. A thesis that promises to describe the similarities between apples and oranges, on the other hand, is interesting and arguable since most people will agree that the similarities are not easily seen.

- *Appropriate.* If the thesis does not follow the assignment requirements, the final paper will not follow the assignment requirements either. Take a few minutes to verify that the thesis follows the assignment by turning the assignment prompt into a question and making sure the thesis answers the question.

- *Short.* Successful students try to keep their thesis statements at ten words or less. This helps you think in-depth about what you want to say and what you want to cover in your paper. While it may seem tedious to do this, it is an important planning step that will pay off immensely later in the assignment process.

Writing process

The writing process should be used regardless of the type of assignment because it can easily apply to papers, speeches, presentation and projects. Follow this writing process for all of your assignments:

Step One: Think about the assignment. Read through the assignment description and start thinking about the requirements and topics before you do any physical work on the assignment. This part of the process allows you to think about possible topics as well as what angle you want to cover on the topic.

Step Two: Brainstorm and write a working outline. During this step, write down all of the information you can think of about the topic as well as questions you have that will require research. Once you have brainstormed, take the information and organize it into several main points. This is a working outline and it may be changed throughout the process. It mostly serves as a way to get started.

Brainstorming Techniques:
Successful students use a variety of brainstorming techniques to explore their topics.

Freewriting	Freewriting is a technique where you spend a set amount of time constantly writing about the topic. When freewriting, it is important to just write and not worry about sentences, complete thoughts or grammar, spelling, or other mechanics. The important thing is to simply write whatever comes to mind regardless if it is on topic or not. If nothing comes to mind, write "I can't think of anything to write" until something else comes to mind. After the time limit, go back and read through the writing and highlight any relevant ideas. Use these ideas as starting points for the assignment.
Listing	Listing is a brainstorming technique where you simply list everything you can think of about the topic. This can be one large list or it can be broken down into sub-topics.

Visual Depictions	Visual depictions have you creating maps, webs, or clusters of the information about the topic. This technique starts with the topic in the middle and the information around the outside. You can use lines and circles to connect related ideas to create the clusters or Web effect.
Cubing	Cubing is a brainstorming technique that requires you to do six specific tasks with the topic: describe it, compare/contrast it, associate it, analyze it, apply it, and argue for or against it.
Reporting	Reporting has you act as a reporter and look for answers to the six journalistic questions: Who? What? Where? When? Why? and How? Use this technique to get a good sense of what areas of the topic you need to research and what areas you are more familiar with.
Utilize Resources	When all other methods of brainstorming fail, turn to the reference section at the library. Here, the dictionaries, thesaurus, and encyclopedias are great starting points to help get the ideas flowing.

Step Three: Write the thesis. At this point, you have spent time thinking and writing about the topic. Now is the time to narrow the information to one concise, arguable, and interesting thesis statement. After writing the thesis statement, go back to the working outline to see if any of the main points needs to be changed, moved, or deleted.

Step Four: Research. Spend time researching the topic. Because the thesis statement sets the paper up to be both interesting and arguable, the researching stage is important for you to find information about each of the main points to fully explain them. There should be two to three resources for each main point. If this is an assignment that does not require research, spend this time brainstorming specific ideas and information for each main point.

Step Five: Write a detailed outline. This is the stage where you read through your research, take notes, and plug the information into the working outline. It will likely involve a lot of going back and forth from notes to your research materials and your outline, but spending time on this will produce a nice, solid outline that will help in the next step immensely.

Step Six: Write. A problem for many students is that they often get distracted while writing their rough draft. The most important thing to remember is that this is a rough draft and the main idea of this step is to get the ideas on paper in a relatively organized and comprehensible manner. Here are some ways to help you do this:

- Use only the outline to aid in writing to keep the focus on the writing and not additional research.

- Plan time to write the entire paper in one sitting.

- Find a quiet place with no internet usage or other distractions.

Step Seven: Put it away. You can get frazzled while working on an assignment constantly. It can be helpful to write the first draft and then put it away for a couple of days. Of course, this does require planning so that you have a couple of days to do this before the assignment deadline, but most successful students will tell you it is worth it in the end because it gives them a fresh look at the assignment when they go back to finalize everything.

Step Eight: Finalize the assignment. After the assignment has "rested" for a few days, revise it. This involves looking for grammatical errors and typos as well as the cohesiveness of ideas. This is also a great time to look for wordiness and redundancy to make the assignment as concise as possible.

At this point, it is important to double-check the conclusion. Many students tend to skimp on the conclusion because they are tired of the assignment by the time they get to the end or want to rush to get it done. By putting it away for a few days, you can take a fresh look at the conclusion.

Once the assignment is finalized, you need to think about the method of how you will present the assignment to the professor:

- Double-check hard copies to ensure that the printing is readable and contains all of the pages.

- Clearly label papers that will be turned in electronically.

- Practice speeches and presentations. Use visual aids during rehearsal if applicable.

- Prepare and double-check audience handouts for accuracy, correctness, and proper grammar. Make sure there are enough for the size of the audience.

- Double-check all projects that have multiple mediums to make sure everything is in its proper place.

Other considerations for projects, papers, and presentation

Tip #90

Keep in mind other considerations while completing assignments. Professors will notice the little things that make one student's assignment stand out from the rest — for better or worse.

If you follow these guidelines, you can help ensure your assignments will stand out for the better:

- *Know the audience.* There will be times when the intended audience will be specified in the assignment prompt. When there is no specified audience, you should complete the assignment for the students instead of the professor so you do not leave out important details that the professor may be checking for in the grading of the assignment. For example, if the students in a child development class are asked to make presentations about birth defects, they will want to give information that will be beneficial to the students in the audience and not the professor, who arguably already knows much of the information about the birth defects. Even though the professor will be grading the assignment, in most cases, it is best to assume the audience is really the class — they have general knowledge of the topic but may need background in certain areas to fully understand the information.

- *Cite sources.* When in doubt, it is always better to cite than to not cite and end up plagiarizing something from a source. Additionally, many colleges and universities use plagiarism detection programs that help professors detect blatant copying of information. If you are not sure about how to cite your sources you should consult with your professor on the preferred citation method for the assignment.

- *Use proper grammar.* The same lingo used in email and texting is not appropriate for college-level assignments.

- *Be neat.* Neatness and appearance can make a big impression. Rumpled, folded, or badly printed papers do not make a good impression. All assignments that are turned in in-person should look professional and neat to show that you care about the assignment and the class.

Part V: Avoiding Studying Downfalls: How to Keep Up With It All

Even the most successful, studious, and conscientious students will find themselves in situations that require extra help. There will be semesters that require obscene amounts of writing because of the mix of classes and there will be semesters that require tons of reading because of the mix of classes. There will also be semesters that are difficult because all of the classes are extremely demanding. When this happens, all students, even the most successful ones, need to know what to do to survive and succeed.

Chapter 13

Balancing Your Life

One of the best parts of college is becoming involved in an extracurricular activity. Extracurricular activities are school-sponsored organizations such as student government, athletics, academic clubs and organizations, service groups, and multicultural groups. Depending on the organization, time commitment can be as little as an hour or two each month to as much as 10 or more hours per week. Students who partake in extracurricular activities find they have to do some fancy scheduling and make an extra effort to get everything done, but most will agree it is worth the effort. Extracurricular activities not only foster a sense of school pride, but they also teach real-world skills, enhance experiences, develop self-awareness, and look great on a resume.

Avoid Procrastinating

When it comes to participating in extracurricular activities, you'll find that one of the biggest downfalls is procrastination. You may have so much to do that there is not time to waste time. The best way to avoid this is to stick to a study schedule as well as to schedule free time so it does not get overlooked in the way of "all the other stuff."

Make a list of priorities

If you can successfully balance all of your activities, then you clearly know your priorities and are able to make quick decisions based on them. For example, a student athlete puts her sport as one of her top priorities. To be able to continue competing she knows that she needs to keep up with her grades. This helps her overcome distractions when she is supposed to be studying. Another student may be on the student government. He knows he needs to stay healthy to be able to function well. During busy weeks, it is easy for him to say no to his normal workout in lieu of something else, but he knows if he does he will feel crummy by the end of the day and will be less productive. So, the priority of feeling healthy helps him keep his scheduled workout.

Get a tutor

If you are involved in time-consuming extracurricular activities, you do not have time to mess around. If you are struggling in a class or think you may struggle in a subject, you need to explore the tutoring options offered at your university.

Tip #91

Universities often have a variety of tutoring options from a one-time thing to regular, weekly sessions. This scheduled tutoring time ensures you will get the help you need when you need it instead of spending precious time struggling with the topic on your own.

Utilize university-enforced study sessions

Extracurricular activities that are time consuming, such as sports, often have team or university-enforced study sessions. Students are required to attend, but of course no one can actually make them sit down and productively study. Use this time to your advantage and study! Make sure you come prepared with a variety of work and get down to business so that when the session is over you can take a break and reward yourself for a job well done.

Balance Work and School

While it would be nice if every college student said, "school comes first and my job is secondary," this is not the case for everyone. Some students have families to support and others simply could not afford their tuition and living expenses if they did not also have a job, so it is fair to say that, in some cases, school and the job go hand-in-hand.

Regardless of why they have a job, many students think it would be ideal to be able to attend college without having to have one. Others have found that having a job helps them stay on task when they are studying and use their scheduled work times as a great motivator to get things done when they have the time. Either way, students who have jobs need to take extra care to balance it with their schoolwork.

Look for on-campus jobs

One way successful students balance school and work is to look for jobs on campus. These jobs are often more flexible than other jobs, and sometimes the hours can fit in between classes throughout the day. Plus, if you work on campus, you do not waste time commuting to a job elsewhere. There are many types of jobs available to students on most campuses:

- Food service

- Grounds keeping

- Security

- Libraries

- Janitorial services

- Professor and program assistants

- Department aides

- Fitness centers

- Daycare centers

- Computer labs

- IT services

- Printing and copying centers

- Bookstores

- Residence halls

- Research assistants

- Tutoring

Stay organized to study anywhere

If you work while going to school, understand that you need to be prepared to study during any spare time. This could be on the bus on the way to work, at work if it is slow, or during a spare 15 minutes when a lecture was let out early.

Tip #92

Always carry study materials with you.

You also need to know where you are going to be and what you need to do. This requires you to keep a detailed schedule of work, classes, and study sessions. Successful working students also know they need to schedule free time so that they do not become burned out from constantly working.

Cut back as needed

Even the most organized student will need to cut back working hours at certain times of the semester to be able to be successful in the classroom. Midterms and finals, if they fall in close proximity in the same class, are often stressful weeks for every student. If you work, you'll want to discuss this with your employer about switching hours or taking time off to allow for the most studying time possible.

Chapter 14

Keeping It Real

College can be so overwhelming for students that they may soon find themselves doing what needs to be done to get by. This is all right once in awhile to get through stressful times, but students who constantly have to do this may find they are not reaching their full potential. Because college is a time of maturing as much as it is a time of earning a degree, successful students have taken the time to make sure they stay true to themselves.

Examine Values

Take the time to examine your values. This could be as simple as making sure you are spending enough time with your friends and family to as drastic as making sure you are being honest in your work. By examining your values, you help yourself stay true to your priorities — this helps you stay motivated because you know you are on the right track.

One way you can examine your values is by making sure you have your priorities in order. If they are not, you need to make changes to your daily life. You can also evaluate if what you are doing makes you happy. If not, you need to figure out what you need to change.

Define Personal Success

Students also need to define for themselves at what point they will be successful. For some, it is earning straight A's in college and graduating with high honors. For others, personal success is earning their degree but also completing a certain type of volunteer work. Other students may deem themselves successful if they have made an impact on the campus or student body while in school. Personal success is different for everyone and those who define it for themselves will be able to judge whether or not they are successful students.

Make Goals

Many students avoid setting goals because they do not know what they want out of college, they don't know how to set goals, or they simply get too overwhelmed with the idea of setting goals and then having to stick to them. It is important for you to remember, however, that goals can be modified or scrapped as your life changes. Goals are invaluable for getting you in the correct mindset to become productive.

- Goals help with motivation because they give you an endpoint to work toward.

- Goals help you make difficult decisions. If the decision hinders progress toward an important goal, it is probably the wrong decision.

- Goals help you with your priorities. Again, if something hinders progress toward a goal, it most likely should not be high on the priority list.

Setting goals can be overwhelming, but here are a few tips to use when setting goals:

- The goal needs to be desirable to you. Too often, students set goals because they sound good or they think they will make others happy. These goals will often fall by the wayside and will often not be big motivators if you don't want to reach them anyway.

- The goal needs to be achieved in connection with other goals. For example, a full-time student who has one goal of graduating in four years will likely not be able to fulfill a goal that requires them to work a full forty-hour week as well. These two items are not compatible with one another.

- The goals should be positive and explain what you want to do, not what you want to avoid.

- The goals should be specific so you will know when you reach them.

- The goals should be written down on paper and kept visible such as on a bulletin board or on a homepage on the internet.

Stay Connected to Reality

Students who live and work on campus can easily lose sight of the real world. It is easy to work, study, and go to class without really paying attention to what is going on in the real world unless a professor brings up a current event.

Tip #93

Make an effort to read the newspaper, current event magazines, news sites on the internet, or watch news programs at least once a week to keep in touch with what is happening in the world around you. Listening to NPR is a professor favorite.

If nothing else, keeping in touch with current events will help you apply the concepts you learn in class in a broader sense—not just what is happening on campus.

Examine Majors and Minors Frequently

Students often start college with an idea of what they want to do when they are finished. The number of students who actually finish with their first major is quite low. It is not unusual for students to change majors, decide on a double major, or add an extra minor during their education. Most students would probably agree it is better to add an extra semester of schooling to change a major than to finish with a degree they do not want to use. Look for the following signs that you may be in the wrong major:

- You are making the best of the situation because you are not enjoying what you are studying.

- You do not enjoy many (or any) of your classes in your major(s).

- You cannot decide on a job that you would both be qualified for and enjoy.

- You tried an internship and were miserable.

- You do not feel challenged.

- You complain about your studies a lot.

- You feel like fellow classmates are much more interested in the subject matter than you are.

- Your priorities have changed and the current major no longer helps you work toward meeting your goals.

Know When to Transfer

It is not unusual for students to transfer from one university to another to finish their schooling. There are many reasons for the transfer including being closer to home, being at the same school as a significant other, finding a school that has a better program for their intended major, or simply wanting a change of scenery.

Tip #94

If you're at a crossroads and can't make the call of whether to transfer or not, here are some strong indicators that you should take steps to transfer to another school:

- A different school has a more prestigious program for your intended major.

- The only reason you're not changing majors is that your current school does not offer the major you want.

- The current school is becoming unaffordable.

There are also reasons why a college transfer is not necessarily the best choice. If you are having a difficult time adjusting to college life, you may think it will be easier at a different school, but sometimes what you need is to just give it a little time. Also, you may be looking at transferring to a new school to be closer to friends. While this is not necessarily a bad idea, it could be if the new school does not have the right program for you.

Once the decision to transfer has been made, for whatever reason, it is important that you take your time so you can be sure to find the right school.

Chapter 15

Mental Fortitude

oncentration and memory. Too bad you can't just order large quantities of these mental capacities on Amazon, huh? The toughest part is that college requires a lot of it, and it's easy to get drained. This chapter will first lay out ways that will improve your focus and then strategies for improving memory.

Keep a List

One of the biggest reasons students have difficulty concentrating is that they start thinking about the other things they need to get done.

Tip #95

Make a list of everything so you can concentrate in the here and now.

This could be what you need to get at the grocery store or ideas for your next project. It could also be about who you need to email and why. Successful students have found that when their minds start wandering when they need to be studying or when they are sitting in class, the best thing for them to do is to keep a notebook handy so they can make a list of whatever is trying to take over their thoughts. If you keep thinking about the grocery store, quickly make a list. If you keep thinking about that email, then make a list of who you want to email when you are done. That way, you know the list is waiting for you and you can stop thinking about it.

Remove External Distractions

Another common cause of a lack of concentration is the external distractions that pull your attention away from the subject. Students who sit near a door may get distracted by noise in the hallway, or students sitting near windows may get distracted by the outdoors. Some students even sitting in the back of the class may get distracted by other students in class. The solution? Sit at or near the front of the class.

External distractions while studying can be household chores, roommates, television, and the internet. You can avoid these by not studying at home and staying away from the internet. You can also look for quiet places to study that do not have a lot of traffic that could potentially add another distraction.

Avoid Multi-Tasking

Reading and walking on the treadmill may sound like a great idea when you get started, but it's a lose-lose situation. You don't really learn much, and you don't really get a great workout. Multi-tasking sounds like a great concept and those who multitask may get more done, but not done as well as if they had concentrated on just one task at a time.

Set Mini-Goals When Concentration is at Its Worst

If you have a difficult time concentrating, you may also want to try setting mini-goals to help you get your work accomplished. They're comparable to small stages in a videogame, or completing sections of a puzzle. Here is how it works:

- *A mini-goal* should be accomplishable in a relatively short amount of time (10 to 15 minutes).

- *It should be specific.* "Read more for the next few minutes" is not specific. "Read the next section in the chapter and answer the relevant questions on the study guide" is extremely specific. Being specific will activate your drive to complete concrete goals.

- *There should be a reward.* Take a break, have a snack, check email, or chat with a friend. The reward should be quick as well so you can get back on task for the next mini-goal.

A whole series of mini-goals will accomplish more than simply saying "I need to read this entire chapter" and daydreaming the whole time. By breaking up one massive goal into a larger list of smaller goals, you're accomplishing more!

When All Else Fails...

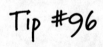
Tip #96

Take a break.

The lack of concentration is your brain telling you that it needs a break, so listen to it. Go do something else *completely different.* Your brain is over-stuffed and needs to rest and digest. Go satisfy some other needs by doing something physical, like cleaning up, walking to the grocery store, finding something on campus to do—whatever shakes up your routine.

Exercise the Brain

Your brain will function better if it is exercised on a regular basis. College students may argue that their brains are exercised enough as it is, but there are games out there that are genuinely fun and make your brain more elastic and able to retain information. You might have already dabbled in crossword puzzles or logic games, but you'll be surprised to learn that even select video games can be really good for your brain. An article in the Huffington Post cited studies showing that video games can stimulate growth in the areas in your brain related to memory, relieve stress and depression, and slow the brain's natural aging process. The key, as with anything, is moderation.

Chanting, Repeating, and Reciting

One of the best ways to remember things is to practice the repeat and recite method. This can be practiced with little things such as a grocery list or a list of supplies in your backpack. Practicing with incidental items will help you be able to use the repeat and recite method while studying.

Tip #97

For studying, you can use flash cards and other active studying strategies, but you should be working in an area where you can audibly recite the information to help you remember it. In this way, you create a sense that someone is talking to you about the information, making it easier to remember. While you're reciting, try talking about the information to yourself and why it's important.

Create Acronyms

If you are trying to remember a specific list or words, the steps to a procedure, or a specific theory or rule, you can use acronyms. Acronyms take the first letter of each word (or important word) and create a word or short phrase out of the initials. Once you have studied the acronym a few times, you will remember the words that go along with each initial. Here are some examples:

- F.A.C.E.: This can help music students remember the spaces on the treble staff. Once they know this, they can fill in the notes for the lines as well.

- H.O.M.E.S.: The names of the Great Lakes: Huron, Ontario, Michigan, Erie, and Superior.

Visualize the Information

If you can put a vibrant or outrageous visual with the material, you will be able to remember the information through the visualization. For example, when trying to remember the capitol of Pennsylvania, you may make the visualization of a big, hairy pen and think of the sentence, My HARR-y PENN is BiG to help you remember Harrisburg, Pennsylvania.

Another example of this theory is associating a person's name with his or her appearance. It can help you recall other people's names and can be successful as long as you do not share your associations with the named person. Obviously, you don't call "Harry" a "hairy guy" or call "Ruby" a "rube." You can do this with important historical figures you're learning about in class as well.

This principle can be applied to any topic, but it works best when you have to associate information with a keyword or phrase such as a date and its events or a person and his or her significance. As long as the picture is outrageous enough to stand out in your memory and has enough clues to be associated with the right keywords, it will be a great way to help remember the clues. The downfall is that it takes time to come up with visualizations, but this skill becomes easier with practice.

Rhyme to Remember

Fun Fact

Did you know we're more likely not only to *remember*, but to *believe* something if it rhymes? That's why there are so many commercials that create rhymes to get customers to believe their company's products are better.

There are times when a simple rhyme that explains the rule or date will help you. There are many of these rhymes already in use but you may also want to make up your own to make it relevant to the topic you are studying. For example:

- "I" before "E" except after "C" or when sounded like "A" as in neighbor or weigh.

- In fourteen-hundred-and-ninety-two, Columbus sailed the ocean blue.

Overload the Senses

A final way to help improve memory is to overload the senses. What this means is when you have important information to remember for an exam, you should apply the information to as many senses as possible. The more senses you involve in studying the information, the more likely you are to remember it. An example is to create a visualization of the material, link it to a tangible object, and imagine what it smells like. By doing this, you can recall the image, the tangible object, or the smell and will likely recall the information that goes with it.

Chapter 16

Loving Words

I n college, your best friend isn't your roommate. It isn't your friend you sit next to in your astronomy class. It isn't your dog, even. It's language. Words are, in essence, only useful as labels for things and concepts that grow more complex the more you get educated. The more you improve your language, the more you improve your knowledge. And vice versa. Here are some quick tips on how to do just that.

Word-of-the-Day Emails or Fancy Vocabulary Builders

Since most students are online at least once a day anyway, some students subscribe to a word-of-the-day email so they have easy access to a new word each day. The key to making this work is reading the email and usage examples and then making it a point to use the word at least once each day (more if possible). Plus, a word can open up so many doors to history and culture. Take this fascinating word from Dictionary.com's word-of-the-day email:

"Faustian
\FOU-stee-uh n\
adjective
1. sacrificing spiritual values for power, knowledge, or material gain: a Faustian pact with the Devil.
2. of, relating to, or characteristic of Faust: a Faustian novel."

Or, look into getting a Vocabulary Builder. *Merriam-Webster's Vocabulary Builder* is a great one, and at the end of every section which covers different Greek or Latin Roots, they have a list of words that stem directly from Greek mythology with definitions that include the story of their origins. You can learn about Homer's *Odyssey*, the sirens that wrecked the sailor's ships, or sibyls, fortune-tellers that were esteemed in ancient Greece. Keep notes about these words and their origins and dazzle your professors and fellow students with a masterful vocabulary!

Another great way to keep your vocabulary strong is to challenge your mom to a game of Words with Friends. We have faith in you.

Master Roots, Prefixes, and Suffixes

Much of the English language is based on Greek and Latin roots. Additionally, many words contain prefixes and suffixes that are common to the language. People who understand the meaning of these roots, prefixes, and suffixes can decipher the general meaning of new words without consulting a dictionary. Here are some examples:

Some Greek and Latin roots, prefixes, and suffixes

- Ali: Other. Alias, Alibi.

- Amor: Love, Liking. Amorous, Enamored.

- Dura: Lasting. Duration.

- Vive: Life. Revive, Vivid.

- Ambi-: Both. Ambidextrous.

- Con-: With. Connected, Conspire.

- Inter-: Between. Interstate.

- Mono-: One. Monologue, Monogamy.

- -Cide: Kill. Suicide.

- -Ectomy: Cut. Appendectomy.

Keep a List of New Words

Students who are serious about learning new words keep a list of new words that they encounter so they can look them up in the dictionary.

Tip #98

Keep this list in a notebook so you have room to write in the definition as well as examples of usage. This way, you can study these new words and become familiar enough with them to actually use them.

Read

You must be exposed to a word several times before you will be able to remember it and use it properly. The more you read, the more words you will learn. Again, check out a vocabulary builder, or read a nonfiction book that's closely related to what you're studying in college. This way, you will likely hear the words and concepts you learned from the book in your classes.

Stay Motivated

*C*ollege is difficult, especially if you're in a particularly rigorous university. You may even want to throw in the towel sometimes. Just remember that if you think college is hard, life only continues to get more difficult afterwards. College is an opportunity to *grow* to become stronger so you can tackle the obstacles that lie ahead. It's easy to get overwhelmed, but you might need to do some self-examination if you're taking "a night off" *every* night, or you're finding it hard to wake up in the morning.

Tackle the Source of Your Lack of Motivation

Learn to always look for the source of your problems instead of the symptoms. If you're feeling blue about studying, ask yourself why that might be the case, instead of jumping to make some coffee or trying to watch television to cheer you up. Once you know the source, the rest will follow. A lack of motivation can signify any number of things, including:

- Not being interested in the classes may mean you need to reevaluate your course of study.

- Not enjoying a particular class may mean you need to decide if you need to be taking the class. If it is not required, it may be worth dropping it.

- Being exhausted. You need to reorganize your schedule or adopt healthier habits.

- Personal or relationship issues may mean that you should look into counseling.

Tip #99

Remember that there are millions of people your age who have their trials and tribulations in college that cause them to feel depressed or unmotivated. Everyone is bound to deal with them in a unique way, but never doubt the power of self-examination.

Do you have a lot of unnecessary fears that are holding you back? Are you taking certain classes to please your family, but not yourself? Do a bit of self-questioning and find out ways to help yourself.

Learning Self-Reliance

An important lesson that most students learn early on is they cannot rely on other people to motivate, remind, or force them to get their work done. Some students, especially first-year students, struggle with the adjustment process of no longer being monitored by their parents or teachers. Additionally, college professors don't hound students to get their work done or call them in for meetings if it looks like they are falling behind like high school teachers do.

Tip #100

Use your inner resources! It's a good thing. While everyone needs to be around supportive and loving people, when you're an adult, you don't rely on these people to keep you accountable for your actions. If you're having trouble with this, make sure to make friends with very independent students. Study with them. Watch them, and learn.

Make Lists

Maybe you work best when you can visualize what you have done and what you have left to do. A great motivator for you may be to write lists like the one mentioned at the very beginning of the book.

You don't have to do it on just a bland piece of white paper either. There are a lot of ways to make college like a "game" in some respects.

Some students get a fat stack of multi-colored post-its. They assign colors to their classes (green for chemistry, yellow for literature, pink for Spanish, etc.) and break down, step-by-step, the tasks they need to get done for each class.

They put the **hardest work** first, laying them out on the table. Once they complete everything for a class, they rip the post-it off and throw it away.

Of course, there are probably a million ways to make lists. You can try on-line methods, or use alarms to give yourself a time limit for each list. Experiment, collect data, and use what works!

Start Small

Even with all of these great tips, sometimes the most successful students are unable to motivate themselves to do what needs to be done. This is when it is time for you to trick yourself into working.

Tip #101

Start small when you have a lot on your plate. Taking your tasks on one at a time will make it all much more manageable.

Here is how it works:

A successful student may put off starting an assignment for a variety of reasons. She knows she needs to at least get a start on it, but it is her evening to relax. She has about 25 minutes until her favorite live comedy show comes on. Here's where the student "tricks" herself, by using this very small, but very useful, window of time to plan out how she'll get the assignment done. She knows if she gets right on task, she can have her plan of action done within about 15 minutes. She finds her materials, sits down at the table, and begins reading the assignment sheet.

At this point, one of three things can happen:

- *Situation A.* The student reads through the sheet, jots down questions, and makes a plan. She is done within 15 minutes and has a solid idea of what needs to be done to complete the project. Plus, she knows what she needs to be thinking about to get the project going.

- *Situation B.* The student reads through the sheet, jots down questions, and makes a plan. Then, she realizes she already knows what prompt she wants to use because one popped out at her when she was reading through them. In addition, she initially thought about three possible topics that may work depending on the information available. She looks at the clock and sees she still has 10 minutes until her show starts, so she gets on the library's online catalog to see what types of information would be available for her possible topics to help her decide. She knows she does not need to make her decision right away, but she has things to think about to get the project moving in her brain.

- *Situation C.* The student reads through the sheet, but as she is doing so, she realizes she does not understand the prompt and how it relates to the course and the topics discussed in class. She writes several questions on the sheet as she reads through it and then double-checks her professor's office hours to see when she can plan to go ask him or her about the assignment.

Whichever situation occurred, the student accomplished something that night. In situation B, she tricked herself into completing more than she planned. In situation C, she was relieved she had taken the time to read through the assignment sheet so she would have enough time to schedule a meeting with the professor.

Conclusion

I f you've read the entire book, congratulations on graduating from "study-ing strategies 101." But just as you can read words on a page and take nothing from it, we sincerely hope you've excavated some gold nuggets from this book. Although this book is focused on studying methods and college tips, it's written with perhaps an even more important motive: to get you to become a well-rounded person. Becoming a good student is more than about having a glossy GPA (which, unless you want to go to graduate school, won't actually matter that much) — it's about growing, gaining knowledge for things you're passionate about, and being exposed to things that amaze you. Being a good student will relax you and open you up to life both in and outside of college.

So, now that you've read the book, it's up to you to decide what student you want to be. You can be the perfectionist who's landlocked at the library. You can party all the time and try to get a spot on MTV's "Spring Break." Or, you can be the student who uses strategies for their tests and assign-ments, balances their life, and organizes themselves and their time in a way that opens all kinds of doors to walk through. Throughout it all, never lose sight of who you are and what you want in life. We hope this book has only helped you move closer towards fully satisfying and realizing your purpose as you begin this exciting chapter of your life.

Happy studying!

Glossary

Acronym: an abbreviation formed from the initial letters of other words and pronounced as a word (i.e. NASA, NABISCO).

Active Learning: is a process whereby students engage in activities, such as reading, writing, discussion, or problem solving that promote analysis, synthesis, and evaluation of class content.

Aural: of or relating to the ear or the sense of hearing.

Bibliotherapist: is an expressive therapy that involves the reading of specific texts with the purpose of healing.

Cubing: a brainstorming technique that requires the student to do six specific tasks with the topic: describe it, compare/contrast it, associate it, analyze it, apply it, and argue for or against it.

Depiction: the action or result of showing or representing something, as in art.

Directive: an official or authoritative instruction.

Fortitude: courage in pain or adversity.

Freewriting: is a technique where the student spends a set amount of time constantly writing about the topic. When freewriting, it is important to just write and not worry about sentences, complete thoughts or grammar, spelling, or other mechanics.

Intuitive: using or based on what one feels to be true even without conscious reasoning; instinctive.

Lateral Thinking: is solving problems through an indirect and creative approach, using reasoning that is not immediately obvious and involving ideas that may not be obtainable by using only traditional step-by-step logic. The term was coined in 1967 by Edward de Bono.

Listing: is a brainstorming technique where the student simply lists everything he or she can think of about the topic. This can be one large list or it can be broken down into sub-topics.

Major: your main specialization or area of study in school.

Minor: your secondary specialization or area of study in school.

Mirroring: is the behavior in which one person subconsciously imitates the gesture, speech pattern, or attitude of another. Mirroring often occurs in social situations, particularly in the company of close friends or family.

Notate: to write something.

Objective: (of a person or their judgment) not influenced by personal feelings or opinions in considering and representing facts.

Priorities: things that take precedence over, such as personal goals.

Procrastination: the action of delaying or postponing something.

Reflective Learning: is a way of allowing students to step back from their learning experience to help them develop critical thinking skills and improve on future performance by analyzing their experience.

Reporting: the student acts as a reporter and looks for answers to the six journalistic questions: Who? What? Where? When? Why? and How?

Subjective: based on or influenced by personal feelings, tastes, or opinions.

Transferring: when a student moves from one school to another for a better-quality program, personal preference, or a change of scenery.

Tutor: someone who coaches you in an area of study.

Vertical Thinking: is a type of approach to problems that usually involves one being selective, analytical, and sequential. It could be said that it is the opposite of lateral thinking.

Visual Depictions: student creates maps, webs, or clusters of the information about a topic. This technique starts with the topic in the middle and the information expanding around the outside.

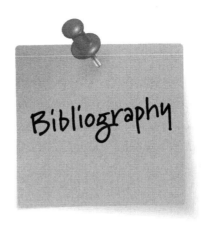
Bibliography

"Emotion Commands Attention and Affects Memory." *Design for Emotion: A Book about Emotional Design*. Web. 06 Dec. 2016.

"Learning Styles." *Lake Superior State University*. Web. 15 Dec. 2016.

"Median Annual Earnings of Full-time Year-round Workers 25 to 34 Years Old and Full-time Year-round Workers as a Percentage of the Labor Force, by Sex, Race/ethnicity, and Educational Attainment: Selected Years, 1995 through 2013." Web. 29 Nov. 2016.

"New Studies Find Taking Notes Is Bad For Your Memory." *Panopto Video Platform*. 26 Aug. 2016. Web. 29 Nov. 2016.

"Reading Books Can Make You Happy." *Psychologies*. Web. 30 Nov. 2016.

"Sounds True to Me." *Psychology Today*. Web. 06 Dec. 2016.

Caumont, Andrea. "6 Key Findings about Going to College." *Pew Research Center*. 11 Feb. 2014. Web. 30 Nov. 2016.

Chatfield, Tom. "Why Reading and Writing on Paper Can Be Better for Your Brain." *The Guardian*. Guardian News and Media, 23 Feb. 2015. Web. 30 Nov. 2016.

Currey, Mason, and Mason Currey. *Daily Rituals: How Artists Work*. New York: Alfred A. Knopf, 2013. Print.

Epley, Nicholas. *Mindwise: How We Understand What Others Think, Believe, Feel, and Want*. New York: Alfred A. Knopf, 2014. Print.

Felder, Richard M., and Barbara A. Soloman. "Learning Styles and Strategies." www.ncsu.edu.

Forbes. Forbes Magazine. Web. 01 Dec. 2016.

Guarini, Drew. "9 Ways Video Games Can Actually Be Good For You." *The Huffington Post*. TheHuffingtonPost.com. Web. 06 Dec. 2016.

Jacobs, Lynn F. and Jeremy S. Hyman. *Professor's Guide to Getting Good Grades in College*. (2006). New York: HarperCollins.

Kaufman, Scott Barry, and Carolyn Gregoire. *Wired to Create: Unraveling the Mysteries of the Creative Mind*. New York, NY: Perigee, 2015. Print.

Kingsbury, Alex. "Get in, show up, drop out: Trying to learn why so many college students fail to graduate." *US News & World Report*. November 20, 2005.

Newport, Cal. *How to Become a Straight-A Student: The Unconventional Strategies Real College Students Use to Score High While Studying Less*. (2007). New York: Broadway Books.

----. *How to Win at College: Surprising Secrets for Success from the Country's Top Students*. (2005). New York: Broadway Books.

Pauk, Walter. *How to Study in College 7th Edition*. (2001). New York: Houghton Mifflin.

Reynolds, Jean. *Succeeding in College: Study Skills and Strategies, 2nd Edition* (2002). United States: Prentice Hall.

Stafford, Tom. "Memory: Why Cramming for Tests Often Fails." *BBC.* Web. 02 Dec. 2016.

Van Blerkhom, Dianna L. *College Study Skills: Becoming a Strategic Learner 5th ed.* (2006). United States: Thomson Wadsworth.

Wolpert, Stuart. "Scientists Learn How What You Eat affects Your Brain - and Those of Your Kids." *UCLA Newsroom.* 09 July 2008. Web. 29 Nov. 2016.

Index

About the Author

Melanie Falconer grew up in a sleepy suburban island town, Alameda, in the vibrant Bay Area, California. She's spent the majority of her leisure time at coffee shops either doodling, eating old lasagna, writing, reflecting, and the like. Sometimes, she'll get up on the stage and dance, scream, or stare intensely into the abyss in a play at her local theaters.

She has a B.A. in Language Studies from UC Santa Cruz, which involved taking rigorous courses in linguistics, Spanish, and history. Out of all of her writing projects, "101 Ways to Make Studying Easier" reminded her of college the most, and she enjoyed basking in nostalgia for used up agendas, office hour visits, outings with friends, and learning something new each and every day.